CARRY NATION

ALSO BY ARNOLD MADISON

Drugs and You
Fast Break to Danger
Smoking and You
Think Wild
Treasure Hunting
Vandalism: The Not-So-Senseless Crime
Vigilantism in America

CARRY NATION

ARNOLD MADISON

THOMAS NELSON INC., PUBLISHERS
NASHVILLE   NEW YORK

For Joddy Rajter

who keeps me organized and on schedule

All rights reserved under International and Pan-American Conventions. Published in Nashville, Tennessee, by Thomas Nelson Inc., Publishers, and simultaneously in Don Mills, Ontario, by Thomas Nelson & Sons (Canada) Limited. Manufactured in the United States of America.

First edition

Library of Congress Cataloging in Publication Data

Madison, Arnold.
    Carry Nation.

    Bibliography: p.
    Includes index.
      1. Nation, Carry Amelia Moore, 1846-1911.
2. Prohibitionists—United States—Biography.
HV5232.N3M3   322.4'4'0924 [B]   76-58839
ISBN 0-8407-6540-1

CARRY
NATION

INTRODUCTION

In January 1920, certain people in the United States were gearing themselves for a war, even though the world's most destructive conflict had ended only two years before. The date of the opening battle in this new war would be Saturday, January 17. The time: 12:01 A.M. At that moment the Eighteenth Amendment to the United States Constitution, (or Volstead Act, after Congressman Andrew J. Volstead of Minnesota) the National Prohibition Act would become law. Henceforth, it would be illegal to import, export, manufacture, transport, or sell "intoxicating liquors" in the United States. For many individuals, January 17, 1920, was known as the day of the second Fort Sumter.

Two warring factions readied their supplies and battle plans as the day drew closer: the drinkers and the law enforcers. Those persons who opposed Prohibition were preparing for the dry years ahead. The wealthy bought huge stores of hard liquor and hid the bottles in warehouses and even safe-deposit vaults. Henry Lee describes in his book *How Dry We Were* one industrious group that purchased the entire stock of a small distillery

9

and carted the cases away in dump trucks belonging to a member who was a road contractor. The average citizen who still wanted to drink, however, could hide away only a limited number of bottles and hope that the liquor would last as long as possible.

Grouped on the opposite side were the governmental agencies that would ensure that the new law was obeyed. The Federal Bureau of Internal Revenue appointed Prohibition directors for various states, who in turn hired agents. This force of ill-selected and poorly trained individuals worked with the Coast Guard, Customs, and the Border Patrol to seal off the country from imported alcohol and to make certain no American manufactured or sold the "intoxicating liquors." Though the law was in their favor, the size of this law-enforcement body was hopelessly small. With the approaching onset of Prohibition, only 950 agents worked within the country. They were assisted by fewer than 300 members of the Border Patrol, who were expected to guard almost nineteen thousand miles of land and water borders.

On Monday, January 12, five days before the controversial law would take effect, the Prohibition Bureau in Washington sought to prevent large-scale storage of liquor. The Bureau warned that with the beginning of Prohibition all liquor supplies not in private hands would be seized. Desperately, people transported the hoarded bottles to their homes. Moving vans, cars, and even baby carriages were utilized in the hasty taxiing service. To compound the ridiculousness of certain modes of transportation, the Prohibition Bureau performed its own act of absurdity. A decree was issued stating that if any man was apprehended carrying a forbidden hip flask, his trousers would be classified as a vehicle of transport and therefore would be confiscated.

Viewing the problem more sensibly were the state and local law-enforcement officers throughout the United States. Extra patrolmen and deputies were hired for the fateful Friday that would mark the end of legal drinking. Both those individuals in agreement with the Eighteenth Amendment and those opposing the law expected a night of wild parties and rebellious public intoxication. As the last few days passed, tension grew.

An unexpected force entered the conflict on Friday, January 16. Large sections of the country were buried under a heavy snowfall. High drifts blocked roads, stalling Model T Fords that carried the last precious bottles destined for private homes. People were forced to cancel their final parties. But even in those areas where the weather was decent, the night turned out to be anti-climactic. The expected crowds in bars and at get-togethers failed to materialize.

At midnight, a reporter from the *New York World* stationed himself on Broadway and Forty-second Street, known even then as The Crossroads of the World, hoping to see crowds equivalent to a New Year's Eve mob. Disappointed, he later reported, "Not 200 persons were in sight." The morning edition of *The New York Times* would carry the front-page headline, "John Barleycorn Died Peacefully at the Toll of 12." At 12:05 A.M., a Brooklyn bartender of forty years entered history as one of the first persons to be arrested for selling liquor. For serving a glass of brandy, he was arrested and held on $1000 bail. And, at approximately the same time, a Chinese restaurant near Forty-seventh Street and Broadway was raided.

Nationwide, however, the night was a letdown. No mass arrests were made. No overflowing, hostile crowds guzzled the last liver-searing legal alcohol. Rather than

11

meet Prohibition with fist-shaking defiance, the country seemed almost indifferent to the new era. All across the United States bartenders and party givers wondered where everyone was that night.

The answer is now obvious. Everyone was at home. At first observers of the national picture blamed the poor turnout on the weather and on the fact that people had bid farewell to drinking on New Year's Eve, three weeks before. Later, when perspective was possible, most experts realized that the country was simply worn out by the years-long temperance debate. Since 1808, when the first American temperance society had formed at Saratoga, New York, until the passage of the Eighteenth Amendment, discussions, speeches, and physical confrontations between the two opposing sides had dominated the American scene. Now, at 12:01 A.M. on January 17, 1920, everyone was glad to have the matter settled in some way.

Though numerous organizations had worked for this settlement, one individual had done more to make the country aware of temperance than anyone else: an indomitable woman, who, nine years before Prohibition's beginning, had mounted a public platform for the last time and told the crowd, "I have done what I could." And, by doing what she could, she far surpassed anyone's dreams of what one person alone could accomplish against what seemed then insurmountable odds.

CHAPTER 1

Though Carry Nation was rarely classified as predictable, certain child psychologists might claim that from birth her environmental influences and genetic traits had predestined her path through life.

Garrard County, Kentucky, was the site of the Moore farm when Carry Amelia was born to George and Mary Moore on November 25, 1846. In appearance this section of the state seemed blessedly pastoral. Rich forests of maple, hickory, and magnolia covered the hills, and the valleys and meadows were sheathed in thick grass. The sparkling streams and slow, lazy rivers abounded with fish of many varieties.

Under this peaceful cloak, however, lay brooding emotions, which had dominated the area since its earliest history. The Cherokees and Iroquois had fought desperately, each claiming the land as their own. With the arrival of white settlers, the Indians found a common foe usurping their land. The constant warfare gave rise to the region's nickname, The Dark and Bloody Ground. Long after Indian raids had ceased to be a threat to the pioneers, a miasma of violence hung over Garrard

County. In the 1840's, the area was known for its long-lasting family feuds, which often erupted into senseless attacks and murders over the most minor disagreements.

In counterpoint to this hostility was the deeply religious nature of the county's inhabitants. The first church established in Kentucky was built in Garrard County, and in the early 1800's the McGee Brothers had introduced the western camp meeting, or revival, to the region. The popularity of revival meetings was tremendous with the Kentuckians. These sessions were characterized by the people's outspoken devotion and overt physical manifestations of their spiritual beliefs. Religion here was not the muted, subtle observance that typified other parts of the rapidly growing nation.

Though the Moore family never engaged in the bloody family feuds or attended revival meetings, Carry's father George was a strongly religious man. Alcohol and tobacco were forbidden in the Moore household. Every Sunday George Moore gathered the family's slaves in the dining hall of the ten-room house, where he read the Bible to them, prayed, and sang hymns with them. This tall, handsome, powerfully built man was a mainstay to Carry in her formative years, and she was never to lose her love for him. Years later, she would say, "If I ever had an angel on earth, it was my father."

In part Carry's total reliance on her father's stability may have been due to the temperament of her mother. This was Mary's second marriage, her first to William Caldwell having ended tragically. Influenced by the antislavery movement, Caldwell had moved Mary and their two sons to Illinois, where he freed his slaves. Unfortunately, Caldwell died suddenly, and Mary was forced to return to her father's home in Kentucky. Later

Moore married her and brought her and the two boys to the plantation on Dix River.

Mary was an attractive, statuesque woman, who had pretensions to aristocracy and was given to periods of depression. The furnishings she purchased for the Moore house were expensive and sometimes stretched the budget close to the snapping point. George catered to her extravagant tastes, hoping that her strange moods would pass as time dulled her earlier unhappiness. The melancholia and hallucinations increased, however. Soon after Carry's birth, Mary announced to her family that she was a lady-in-waiting to Queen Victoria. Events moved rapidly in her mind, because within a few days she informed everyone that she was the Queen. At breakfast, she would appear wearing a long, flowing purple gown and a crown of crystal and cut glass. Eventually, she would see the members of the family by appointment only.

Along with the hallucinations, Mary's temper tantrums began to flare with greater frequency. The mere presence of Carry in the house would ignite a fit of scolding and slapping. As a result, the little girl spent considerable time at the homes of her aunts and uncles and grandparents.

The one person Carry loved almost as much as her father was Grandma Moore. The sturdy old lady had been a widow for twenty years, but she remained as bright and happy as a child. Grandma Moore always made Carry feel loved and wanted, an emotion she did not always find at home. But when Carry was almost five, her grandmother died, and the child was not allowed to attend the funeral, which was held in the family graveyard behind the garden. Carry always regretted being denied a final look at Grandma and not being able to kiss the kind woman good-bye. For two weeks, she wept, and she would often sit near the grave, begging God to take her to join Grandma and the angels.

When no relatives were available for Carry to live with, so she would be at a safe distance from her mother, she passed her days in the plantation's slave cabins. An affinity existed between Carry and blacks that would continue throughout her life. Her earliest playmates were a few local children and the sons and daughters of the slaves. The small group of white and black youngsters roamed the riverbanks, where they made mud pies, picked berries, and engaged in Carry's favorite pastime, climbing trees. Carry held a position of authority among her peers—and not just because she was the owner's daughter. She had a dominating personality and always insisted on being the leader and having her own way. When the other children failed to give in to her demands, she would become angry and even more domineering, or even sick.

A neighbor's child of that time later wrote about Carry. "She was inclined to be a tomboy, was very strong willed and absolutely afraid of nothing. . . . Frequently she led us younger children into mischief. I especially recall the martial spirit, and how she used to delight in assuming the role of a conqueror."

The adult blacks were drawn to Carry because they noticed that the girl was often neglected or abused by her mother. Carry was not pretty, but if Mary had been more in touch with reality, she could have softened the child's rather severe appearance. Carry's dark hair was pulled tightly down on either side of a large forehead and cheeks that slanted sharply to a stubborn chin. She had dark, deep-set, shining eyes, which touched the hearts of the slave women with the way they craved affection.

The women made room beside them for Carry to watch as they spun and wove cloth in the Long House overlooking the river. Fascinated by it all, Carry persuaded her father to construct a miniature spinning wheel on which she would spin for hours in the company of the slaves Aunt Eliza, Aunt Judy, and Betsy.

Surrounded by the slaves for most of her formative years, Carry was affected by many of their beliefs. The women would not let her carry any sharp tool such as a hatchet through the house because they believed witches would then swoop down upon her. They also warned her against throwing salt into a fire. This would mean that Carry would return soon as a dead person and would have to pick the grains from the flames. Carry spent many evenings by a log fire, listening to the blacks' strange tales about ghosts and supernatural spells and the eternal punishment reserved for cruel slave masters.

On Sundays, Carry would attend church, frequently sitting in the gallery reserved for slaves. Often she would be so moved by the spiritual message that she would clap and shout and burst into song. The slave women viewed Carry's normal childish spontaneity as evil and tried to reform her. They lectured Carry for hours on the Judgment Day, which they predicted as bleak for a child given to uncontrollable outbursts. The constant threat of dire consequences caused eight-year-old Carry to have headaches, fits of depression, and visions.

One day, after joining with the slaves in a deeply religious rendering of "Let Us Sit Down and Chat With the Angels," Carry went to the family burial ground, where Grandma Moore's grave was. Here the gravestones were set horizontally on masonry, which lifted the slabs about three feet off the ground. Carry stretched out on a large flat piece of marble and traced the carved letters and numbers with her small fingers. In this sequestered, shaded spot, she had her first vision in which she spoke with several angels. The adult Carry later labeled this experience as being the dawn of her young conscience.

Though these early years were at times difficult for the growing girl, the slaves did bestow tremendous affection and love upon her—something she was not receiving from her mother. Years later, when all these people had gone from her life, Carry wrote, ". . . when I had a headache or was otherwise sick, I would wish that one of the old-fashioned colored women would rub me with their plump hands and call me 'Honey Chile,' and would bathe my feet and tuck the cover around me and sit by me, holding my hand, waiting till I fell asleep. . . . I felt lonesome without them."

The Dix River plantation was a fortunate haven of solidarity for Carry, a refuge she would never find again. The ten-room house was a hewed-log dwelling with a parlor decorated with gold-leaf wallpaper and red plush furniture. Outside were gardens of roses and bridal wreath, and the riverbanks abounded with strawberries, raspberries, and currants. Cliffs rose above the river, and Carry would sit for hours on a hidden ledge, looking out over her world, blissfully unaware of the real one.

During these years, events and political forces within the United States were already shaping the conditions with which the mature Carry would have to deal. In 1846, the same year that Carry was born, Maine passed a law forbidding the sale of liquor. Gold was discovered in California when Carry was two. About the same time, California's desire for admission as a state revived the angry question of free states versus slave states, a conflict that continued to grow during the next decade. When Carry was six years old, Harriet Beecher Stowe's *Uncle Tom's Cabin* was published.

The cruelties depicted in that story, however, did not exist on the Moore plantation. Carry continued to pass her days in the company of the slaves, avoiding contact with her mother as much as possible. Her father endured Mary's hallucinations in hopes that her mind would repair itself in some way. To satisfy his wife's conviction that she was Queen Victoria, George ordered a carriage built for Mary. The vehicle was an ostentatious, rubber-tired carriage, with interior upholstery of rich red plush. A pair of magnificent dapple-gray horses with silver-mounted harnesses drew the royal coach. Mary insisted that when she made her journeys, a slave called Big Bill, clad in a scarlet hunting coat, should ride ahead and blast out the news of the Queen's imminent arrival on a long tin horn.

Thus conveyed, Mary would embark on royal visits. One morning she decided to visit the King of Belgium, but returned dismayed when she was unable to locate his palace. Another day she ordered the carriage halted so she might scold a farmer who was cultivating an onion patch. She informed the startled man that such labor did not befit the Duke of Buckingham.

In general, these occurrences were treated tolerantly by the local inhabitants but with a sadness for George, who, they felt, did not deserve such a tribulation. Word was spreading rapidly through Garrard County that Mary's condition was worsening. Close friends of George Moore began to hint that he should consider institutionalizing his wife. Most people knew that two of Mary's brothers and a sister had already been declared legally insane, and her mother was an invalid who refused even to leave her bedroom.

George became increasingly convinced that this public knowledge of his wife's mental history was not beneficial to her, and that if the family moved to an area where Mary's condition was not common gossip, she might improve. Also, the bloody feuding within the country was intensifying. So far, George Moore was well liked and was considered honest in his business transactions, but murderous disputes were known to erupt with seemingly no logical causes. The two thoughts played upon him, and finally he reluctantly decided to sell the Dix River plantation and move to adjacent Boyle County.

On the day before the departure, a huge auction was conducted, during which some slaves and portions of the expensive house furnishings were sold. The new house in Danville would be smaller. According to Carry, her mother became furious when Big Bill was purchased by a neighboring farmer. Mary wanted Big Bill to announce their arrival in the new town on his blaring tin horn.

George reportedly told his wife, "Nobody rides in style this time, my dear. . . . I'm not wanting to make a big show and hullabaloo right off, not till our new neighbors know us better."

The following morning, a long procession of creaking wagons, cows, and squealing pigs began the slow trek through the Kentucky hills to Danville. Being ripped in this way from the security of the plantation and its slaves was to have an unsettling and permanent effect on Carry. Even as they approached the squarish two-story house that was to be their new home, she felt her mother stiffen nervously. Fear made Carry's blood throb in her temples.

CHAPTER 2

Sadly missing the plantation, Carry adapted to her changed life by commandeering a portion of the new house as strictly her own territory, a vantage point that must have reminded her of the hidden ledge above Dix River. Atop the two-story structure was a lookout tower. There Carry would sit for hours, oblivious of the freezing cold or stifling heat, gazing over the rolling Kentucky hills. Here was another perch from which, alone, she could study her world and try to fit her thoughts into a workable pattern.

Considering the depressed mental state of the Moore family members when they had first arrived in Danville, their day-to-day relationships underwent a sudden and remarkable improvement. Mary, caught up with decorating the house, was able to maintain a stable though distant attitude toward Carry. Also, a steady flow of former friends and relatives began knocking on the front door almost before the Moores had unpacked. Mary's delusions slowly faded as she was surrounded by warm and friendly people. Her mode of dress returned to normal, and there were no royal visits made in the fancy carriage. If George had had initial doubts about this move from Garrard County, his concern must have vanished.

Among those who welcomed Mary was the family of her first husband, the Caldwells. Another frequent visitor, a man to whom Carry was strongly attracted, was Dr. Jackson, one of two physicians George Moore had hired on a yearly basis to keep his family and slaves healthy. Doctor Jackson presented Carry with her first doll purchased in a store. The slave women had made many cornhusk playthings for her, but this gift was something special, and Carry was to treasure the precious doll for years.

A second physician, Dr. Smith, often came to the Moore house these days because Mary was now pregnant, and Carry's opinion of this man was unfavorable. She attributed the feeling to two causes. One was a visit she had made to his office in town. All she would remember about that day were the ugly leeches he kept for bleeding patients and the first human skeleton she had ever seen. The sight of the garishly white bones must have summoned back all those frightening tales told by the slaves about death and the fearful Judgment Day. The skeleton may also have reawakened the child's deep feeling for Grandma Moore, dead four years and left behind on what was now a stranger's land.

Dr. Smith also committed a blunder that was so disturbing to the nearly nine-year-old Carry that she would never forget her anger after she learned the truth. When the physician had delivered a baby boy to Mary, he told Carry that he had discovered the baby in a hollow stump. Desperately, Carry spent hours in the nearby woods, searching for a baby who would be her very own, an infant to whom she could talk, and who would be her constant companion. When she did not find a child, she at first believed that God was punishing her in some way. Not until years later, when she was much older, did she realize how she had been deceived. By then the guilt had taken its toll.

More disappointment was to come to the Moore family. At first Mary was a doting mother to the new baby and to Carry's sister Edna. Only Carry seemed to irritate the woman, whether by her stubbornness or her typically childish misbehavior, such as taking a dash of Mary's perfume. As time passed, Mary's irritation turned into anger, and she would lash out at Carry in fits of unreasonable hysterics. As quickly as Mary had improved, she now regressed. Suddenly she hated the farm, and her derisive talk poured forth continually.

Once again, George prayed that a change would benefit his wife, so he sold the house and purchased a farm in Woodford County. Once again, the heartrending process of auctioning belongings and slaves was repeated. And, again, another emotional blow drove Carry to seek her happiness deeper in that inner world where she found her most peaceful moments. True, the happy dreams fought and often lost to guilt and to those images of death and hellfire implanted by the slaves. But for all the darkness and at times even morbidity, Carry still preferred her inner existence to the outer reality.

The Moore family now entered a second cycle almost identical to the one they had just lived through, but this cycle would spin faster and faster, like a runaway wagon wheel rolling downhill.

The reduced procession of animals, slaves, and wagons wound its way to Woodford County. The Moores settled into their new home, and Mary once again acted coherently. George took an active role in civic affairs and was so respected by the local people that he was made a trustee on a board that was building an orphan's home. For the first time, Carry attended Sunday school, which was taught by a wonderfully warm, giving person. Whether it was the affection or the religious messages or both—something touched Carry so deeply that fifty years later she wrote about this teacher, "She planted seeds in my heart that are still bearing fruit." At home, Carry had a new baby brother upon whom Mary showered affection. Once more, the ragged pieces of the lives of the Moore family formed a deceptively happy scene.

And then Mary's hallucinations and outbursts of temper again shattered the fragile picture. Abruptly, she seemed to be on a continual round of regal visits to the surrounding countryside. At night she spent hours weeping in a dark room. In no time at all events had gone full circle, and the Moores readied themselves for still another move. The destination: Belton, Missouri.

Though George Moore had heard encouraging reports about Missouri from relatives who had moved there from Kentucky, his timing and site selection were certainly unfortunate. Belton was situated in the northwest corner of Cass County, close to the Kansas border. The previous year, 1855, several thousand proslavery Missourians had invaded Kansas, an "abolition" state, and attacked the polling places on election day. Seizing the ballot boxes, they set up a proslavery government in Leavenworth, Kansas. In opposition, the free-soilers organized and antislavery government only forty miles from where the Moores were to live.

More armed men from Missouri came across the border, attacking abolitionist newspapers and looting entire towns. Even private homes were burned, and the residents who opposed slavery were murdered. A Missouri mob pillaged the town of Osawatomie, which was only thirty-five miles southwest of where the Moore farm was to be located. This spate of murders spurred John Brown and his gang to scour the countryside, inflicting retribution upon slaveowners. Open war existed between the proslavery forces and the Jayhawkers, who opposed slavery. The state appropriately became known as "bleeding Kansas."

And George Moore, a man whose own home was frequently a battleground, was preparing to move into this land of violent political differences in hopes that his family would find peace and security and serenity.

The journey was to be much longer than the Moores' previous trips, so a larger proportion of their belongings had to be left behind. Carry watched, stricken, as slaves and livestock were placed on the auction block. And a possession that Carry knew her father prized, a six-team wagon, went to the highest bidder. When George suggested selling the rubber-wheeled royal carriage, however, Mary became overwrought and unmanageable. Surrendering to her manic demands, George agreed that she could keep the fancy but now deteriorating vehicle.

The Moores moved northward to board an Ohio riverboat that would carry them downriver to Cairo. From there they would cross the wide state of Missouri. As the long trek began, Carry seemed to have recovered from this latest shock of seeing more of her early life parceled out to strangers. On the outside, she was pleasant and at times even seemed excited, but this shell was dangerously thin, hiding a psyche that had been beaten too savagely, too often, in the last months. She was always ultrasensitive to criticism, and her psychological resources were practically depleted, leaving her mind open to the pounding guilt instilled not only by her mother's attacks but also by the warnings of the slaves she loved so dearly. Intermingled with all this were the memories—of a death, of a conversation with the angels, and of instances when she firmly believed that God had punished her for being evil.

After the Moores' belongings were loaded onto the riverboat, the family found itself confined in tight quarters. Personalities clashed, and tempers flared. Mary nagged the children constantly, singling out Carry for the harshest reprimands. Frantically, Carry sought a haven. Her refuge, ironically, was to be the creaky wagon that had borne "Queen Victoria" on so many visits. The following day, Carry crept into the coach which rested on the bow of the boat. There, alone, her reveries were undisturbed as primeval forests, log cabins, and a brilliant sunset moved past her.

Suddenly, the door was yanked open, and Mary dragged Carry from the carriage, striking her and screaming hysterical gibberish. Mary had been calling for Carry, and when no one could find her, it was feared the child had fallen overboard. Mary was also probably upset when she found that her least-liked child had entered her own dream world. Through a supper that Carry barely touched, Mary continued the scolding, while George sat back after his futile efforts to control his wife had failed.

The following morning Carry remained in bed, suffering cold symptoms, which developed into intestinal fever or, as she later called the illness, "consumption of the bowels." As the boat slowly moved downstream, Carry became seriously ill, and she would remember for the rest of her life hours when she lay alone, sobbing, wishing she were dead. Her father did not stay with her because he was worried about Mary. The family slaves had to watch over the younger children.

When the Moores disembarked in Cairo, a doctor gave Carry medicine, but it did little to counteract the sickness. Setting out on the rough overland journey, George improvised a bed for Carry in the spring wagon, but even so the slow, torturous trip was extremely uncomfortable. Occasionally, Carry raised her head but saw nothing but flat, brown land. As the procession approached the Cass County farm, Carry momentarily believed they had come home to the Dix River plantation. Happiness seized her, but the joy was short-lived. Even in her fevered state, she realized that only the architectural styles of the houses were the same. This was not the plantation. The plantation was gone forever.

There, in Missouri, she was to lie seriously ill for a year, her body refusing to react to ministrations. Her brightest moments were those in which her father came to her and read to her from the Bible. Too often, however, she lay alone, almost forgotten as daily life went on. Her faithful companions were the debilitating thoughts of guilt.

When Carry, at age sixty, was looking back over that period, she wrote, "I have never seen anyone who I thought had committed more sin than I. . . . I never saw the corruption of but one life, one heart—that was mine. I was never so shocked, so disgusted, so disgraced with remorse over any life so much as my own. My heart was the foulest place I ever saw."

George Moore's infrequent visits to his ten-year-old daughter's bedside was not solely his fault. He was suffering the consequences of his decision to move to Belton. Not only did he have to get the farm in running order, but armed bands of marauders were continually approaching the house and asking for food and fodder. Though these visitors included both pro- and anti-slavery bands, the Moore lands were never ravished as were other farmers' properties. Moore described himself as a "Union man but a Southern sympathizer." This ambiguous position seemed to satisfy people on both sides of the slavery question. Actually, George had no fierce convictions on the matter of slavery versus abolition. Although he himself owned slaves, he did not like the institution of slavery. To him, the use of slaves was a purely economic necessity of the times. He did not treat the blacks as mere collateral, however. Moore took a paternal stance toward his slaves, watching over the health of their bodies and their souls.

Perhaps if his paternal attitude toward Carry had been more consuming, her illness might have been alleviated. As it was, Carry was left to the care of the slaves, who kept reminding her that her sickness was due to sin. Repeatedly, the child was informed that her chances of survival were negligible because she was under punishment from an angered God. Thus, Carry was fed more self-blame at a time when her mind was brimming with remorse.

Convinced by church authorities that a return to religion would cleanse the girl of whatever was causing the strange sickness, George asked Carry to attend Sunday school. Never having refused a request of her father, Carry, more dead than alive, allowed herself to be placed in a carriage the following Sunday and brought to church. The minister handed her a small booklet, which explained that the theft of small, unimportant objects was as serious in the eyes of the Lord as the crimes of a hardened criminal.

Carry remembered the perfume and the small pieces

of gaily colored ribbons and bits of lace she had surreptitiously taken from her mother's room to make dresses
for her dolls. "I was greatly shocked to find myself a
thief," she later wrote. The burden of still another accusation caused Carry to weep guiltily and faint. Her
father helped carry her to the wagon, and at home the
emaciated girl was rushed to her bed.

When she awoke, she saw her father gazing at her
sadly. "Carry, unless you love God and pray, you're
going to die and break all our hearts."

Tears welled up in her eyes. "Pa, I do pray. I'll pray
more. I don't want to break your heart."

The next Sunday George Moore again helped Carry
into the family wagon and drove her to the Christian
Church in Jackson County, where a revival meeting was
to be conducted. Since his arrival in Missouri, Moore
had turned to a more expressive form of religion in
hopes that his farm problems and those he had with
warring factions might be stilled.

The trembling, weak girl half walked and was half
carried to a pew in the rear of the church. As the throb-
bing hymns echoed from the rafters, she experienced a
strange exultation. And then the revivalist stepped onto
the platform. The silver-haired preacher had a deep,
sonorous voice, and his fervent sermon emotionally
stirred the girl who, years before, much to the dismay of
the family's slaves, had been unable to refrain from
clapping and singing at even a simple church service.
She began to weep and prayed that God would take her
to his bosom.

At the close of the sermon, the preacher asked for
new converts, beseeching them with open arms to come
forward to find peace of mind and heart.

"At this point I began to weep bitterly, some power

seemed to impel me to go forward," Carry said later. Alone and unassisted, she struggled to her feet and began to move up the aisle. She stumbled once, twice, pulled herself up again, and then slowly, painfully, made her way to the front bench, where she knelt and prayed, still sobbing. "A cousin of mine came up to me at the close of the sermon and said, 'Carry, I believe you know what you are doing.' But I did not. Oh, how I wanted some one to explain it to me!" Dazed, she felt purified and uplifted as though floating above all her unhappiness.

George Moore and the church officials decided Carry's baptism should take place quickly, so the Moores did not return home that night but stayed with Carry's Aunt Jenny and her husband, Ben Robertson. The next morning Carry was weak and dizzy, but she insisted that the baptism be performed because she knew the service meant so much to her father.

Moore drove Carry about two miles to where the preacher waited by an ice-fringed stream. A mist rose from the water that chilly morning, but Carry felt no cold. She waded a few steps into the freezing water and then was lifted bodily and brought to where the water was over her head. Even when she was dunked below the water, she experienced only a golden glow through her weakened body. Quickly, reverently, Carry was baptized, and then rushed to dry land and warm blankets.

In retrospect, Carry wrote, "The little Carry who walked into that water was different from the one who came out."

CHAPTER 3

A nd indeed, the Carry who emerged from the win-
tery baptism did seem to be a completely different
individual. For the next few months she appeared to be
fully recovered and in a position to view her circum-
stances with newfound equanimity. Though the Belton
farm was not the Garrard County plantation, the place
did have its positive aspects. A stream meandered
through the low hills, affording some of the same plea-
sures as Dix River had: berry picking and peaceful, se-
cluded glades. Although there were no cliffs with hidden ledges, there was an underground grotto beneath
the carriage house. In this damp, dark cavern, where a
stream kept the Moore family's milk and butter cool,
Carry found a refuge to supplant those other secret ha-
vens where she had gone to be alone with her inner
conflicts.

Carry also now seemed better able to take her
mother's rejection in stride, more psychologically fit to
withstand the woman's unfairness and to view Mary's
eccentricities with a somewhat mature understanding.

Soon, however, the incessant critical bombardment

again began to weaken her inner supports, and after particularly severe attacks by her mother, Carry would have violent vomiting spells and return to her sickbed for long stretches of time. The family, preconditioned by Mary's brief periods of competency followed by long stretches of erratic behavior, feared that Carry, too, might spend her life alternating between comparative good health and chronic illness.

Spiritually, the twelve-year-old Carry who was now a baptized member of the Christian Church felt strengthened to such a degree that she believed it was her duty to spread the gospel. As her father had done in Garrard County, Carry rounded up the slaves every Sunday afternoon and lectured them about God's goodness and the evil of sin. If she was well, these compulsory sessions took place in the dining room, but if she was experiencing a recurring bout of sickness, the slaves gathered in her bedroom while Carry, propped up by pillows, read from the Bible and warned the blacks what awaited them if they did not repent.

Beyond the Moore farm, the conflict over slavery deepened and turned more violent. In 1858 fellow Kentuckian Abraham Lincoln challenged incumbent Senator Stephen A. Douglas from Illinois for his seat, and the slavery question was the major issue of the campaign. Douglas won the election, but Lincoln won fame. A year later John Brown led his band of abolitionists in a raid on Harpers Ferry, West Virginia, where he was captured and hanged, and subsequently became a martyr. In future years, Carry, who had considered Brown a brave crusader, would proudly refer to herself as "the John Brown of Prohibition."

In December, 1860, after Lincoln had won the presidential election, South Carolina seceded from the

Union. With the formation of the Confederate States of America early in 1861, concern gripped George Moore that Missouri might also secede.

On April 12, 1861, Confederate troops opened fire on Fort Sumter, in Charlestown harbor. Moore viewed the situation with alarm. First, with the increased talk of freedom, discontent had begun to erode his slaves' cooperative attitude. Also, if the Moores had been in a precarious situation before, trapped as they were between proslavery forces and Jawhawkers, the family would now be in the midst of a bloody Civil War battleground. In addition, Moore noticed that members of these marauding bands often stared at fifteen-year-old Carry, and he wondered if the Missouri farm was a safe place for her. Her chronic illness seemed to have had little effect on her physical growth because Carry was six feet tall and had filled out amply.

A remedy for all these worries seemed to be another move for the family. Once again, the Moores sold what they could, raising little money but enough to see them to their destination in Texas. What remained of the household goods and prime stock was gathered together, and the family, which now included six children, climbed into the wagons and Mary's battered old carriage to begin their emigration.

The trip was horrendous, heat, dust, and typhoid fever being their constant traveling companions. During the arduous trip south through Arkansas and Indian country, ten members of the party became seriously ill. Mary collapsed physically as well as emotionally, leaving Carry to shoulder the tremendous family responsibilities. Slipping from wagon to wagon, Carry cared for the ill, helped make her mother comfortable, and saw that her brothers and sister were safe. When the cavalcade reached Grayson County, Texas, where Moore bought a farm, everyone in the family had lost weight, had been blistered by the white-hot sun, and at times had been too ill even to tend to their personal needs. But Carry had blossomed and was now in robust health.

And this contradictory condition continued. Carry quickly found new friends with whom she rode horses. Texas boys, newly recruited, would stop by the farm often. Though not a sympathizer toward the Southern cause, Carry joined sewing circles that transformed gray homespun into uniforms for Confederate soldiers.

At this same time, her mother and father were experiencing serious problems. Mary continued to ail. She wept continually and declared she could not and would not live in this hell of heat and yellow dust any longer. The farm was failing, too. Almost immediately, most of the Moore livestock died. Drought descended on the land like a smothering cloak, shriveling what few cotton plants George had managed to raise. By fall his hope was gone. Only two horses were still alive, and they had no food for the winter.

George felt his only salvation lay in the North, where he could return to the type of farming he knew well. He decided to move back to Missouri. First, however, he had to free his slaves, because Missouri was now a free state. Carry was pleased that these people would now lead free, independent lives, but the act meant the loss of a main source of love, which had supported her since her youngest days. Nevertheless, the timing for the break was perfect. At this point in her life, Carry was ready to leave girlhood behind and accept the responsibilities of an adult. Though she was never to say so, she might have paraphrased her earlier statement and have written: "The little Carry who started the trip to Texas was not the same Carry who returned to Missouri."

George Moore sold what he could, including Mary's now bedraggled royal coach. With only two horses in their possession, the family could not transport both the light spring wagon as well as Mary's carriage. George traded the once-fancy conveyance to a local storekeeper for food and bedding for his family on the trip north. The effect on Mary was drastic. In her mind, she saw the loss of the vehicle as an abdication under threat, and, like a monarch dethroned, she now slipped into lethargy and weeping for what was lost and could never be regained.

If the journey to Texas had been horrendous, the trip back to Missouri was fraught with danger. In Arkansas, the bouncing wagon was overtaken by the Confederate cavalry and had to pull to one side as clanging gun carriages and waves of foot soldiers tramped past them. Two days later, they passed the sad remnants of the same army after it had been badly beaten in the Pea Ridge battle, which the Moores had almost been caught in the middle of. When the wagon neared Missouri, Carry saw more stragglers in bloody, sweat-stained uniforms: Confederate troops who had been paroled back to their homes in Missouri.

As the long trip progressed, and more fire-gutted buildings and dead, rotting corpses of both blue- and gray-clad soldiers were seen, dread replaced hope, and George and Carry began to realize what they should expect when they reached Belton.

Their fears were confirmed as they drove the last half mile to the Cass County farm. Fences were broken down, windows smashed, and inside the house was filled with animal and human filth. Everything that could be moved had been stolen, and what was left behind had been viciously smashed. Even while the Moores were making the house livable, the outlaw bands returned. The Union forces had driven the Confederate troops from the state, but gangs of bushwhackers and copperheads (deserters and outlaws who sympathized with the South) still roved the land. Often, Moore would hide his family in the house while he went out to face the robbers, offering buttermilk, fruit, or other foods to protect what few belongings the family still had.

Within a few months of their arrival, the Moores received word from the Northern commander of that section of Missouri. He ordered all residents to leave their homes and go either to a military post or to Kansas City. The alternative was arrest and possible death.

So even before the Moores had had a chance to settle down, they were uprooted again, this time moving to Kansas City. At first the family was forced to live in a decaying slave cabin, but George soon earned a little money from real-estate sales and was able to provide his wife and children with presentable quarters. Carry attended Mr. and Mrs. Love's boarding school in Liberty, a few miles from home.

The seventeen-year-old girl, lacking a formal education, was an eager student and read every book available, especially the classics and books on history. At the school, Carry also entered into a normal social life. She received gentlemen callers, though her relationship with them was a bit more formal than that of the other school girls. There was no hand-holding, no going on hay rides, no sitting alone in the parlor. For too long and too often, the message had been impressed upon Carry that sex was sinful, and she was at this time too new to social contact to form her own opinions. "I had been taught that to inspire respect—love from a man—you must keep him at a distance. This often made me awkward and reserved; but it did me no harm."

Though Carry kept her suitors at a distance physically, she tried to make contact intellectually. "When I had company, I always directed the conversation so my friend could teach me something, or I could teach him." Carry and her young man would read poetry together, preferably Sir Walter Scott, or discuss history, such as the Golden Age of Greece.

Each week, Carry taught Sunday school; every night she read the Bible and prayed. The prayers, however, were never said in bed, for that would be disrespectful to God. During this period of her life she learned that a proper show of humility during spiritual sessions was "advancing upon your knees," a phrase she was to use throughout her life.

When the war ended, the Moore family moved back to the Belton farm, which was now in ruins. Most of the buildings except for the main house had rotted and collapsed, and the fields that once had yielded rich crops had gone back to scrub. Existence was not a matter of starting over but beginning from scratch, and George Moore was no longer a young man. His wife was ill, and there were no slaves to care for the children and to do household chores. George sent a message to Carry, who had never refused a request from her father, and she left school immediately for Cass County, where she cleaned, cooked, washed clothes, and saw that her brothers and sister went to school.

Life at the farm was far different from the sheltered life at boarding school. The mornings were spent bending over a steaming washtub scrubbing her father's dirt-crusted farm clothing, and in the afternoons she cleaned a house that now seemed unable to keep out the Missouri dust. Evenings, exhausted but not so tired that she neglected her prayers, Carry knelt in a corner of her room facing the wall and began her supplications. Head bowed, she advanced on her knees as had "David, Abraham, Elijah, Paul and Christ." Only when she felt she had impressed her sincere devotion upon the Lord would she allow her aching, tired body to slip between the sheets.

In the fall of 1865, when Carry had bloomed into an attractive young woman, a new guest came to live at the Moore house. George, as in his previous residences, had impressed the local citizens with his honesty and efficiency. Now, as the president of the school board, he had set about hiring a teacher. The successful candidate was Dr. Charles Gloyd, a medical man originally from Vermont, but now a tall, handsome ex-captain of the Union army. Gloyd was extremely knowledgeable, could engage in brilliant conversation, and spoke several languages. He was a type of person Carry had never met, so she had no objective scale against which to measure him.

Mary, however, with her manic craftiness, may have noticed how Gloyd's warm brown eyes frequently sought approval from her daughter. Carry, at this time, took care to improve her appearance. Her eyes were soft, and she wore her brown hair in ringlets. She was full-bosomed and tall and carried herself with assurance. In Mary's opinion, a doctor who had no medical practice and therefore had to teach school was not a worthy prospect for the Queen's daughter. Mary issued an edict that Gloyd and Carry were never to be in the same room unchaperoned. The Belton farmhouse was not a very large structure, and so at times the job of avoiding such a situation meant that Gloyd had to leap up from a chair and run out of a room whenever Carry passed through on her way to the kitchen. Carry appealed to her father to put an end to this ridiculous situation, but George had his own prejudices. He warned Carry that Gloyd was a heavy drinker, which in the Moore household was a capital crime.

The stubbornness that had characterized Carry from birth now dictated her reactions. For one thing, she had never seen Gloyd drunk. For another, his conversations with her were loftily poetic, and she felt that if his love was as true as she believed, that deep feeling would transcend any weakness for alcohol.

So, under the baleful gaze of two chaperons, Carry and Charles engaged in secret note writing. The deposit box was appropriately a volume of Shakespeare's plays and sonnets, which sat on a table in Gloyd's room. They worked out elaborate code words, which were slipped into the breakfast-table conversation. Hearing a key word, Carry waited until Charles had left for school and then sneaked into his room to read the cherished note. Quickly, she penned an answer and slid it into the book to await Gloyd's homecoming that afternoon. Even the elements of the courtship seemed highly romantic to the girl, whose chief knowledge of love up to now had come from reading Sir Walter Scott.

Charles Gloyd's contract was not renewed at the end of the school term, so he moved to Holden, a town in nearby Johnson County, where he started a medical practice. Before he left, Gloyd told Carry that they would soon be married. Meanwhile, he sent for his parents and began acquiring a respectable list of patients.

George Moore occasionally journeyed to Holden in connection with his real-estate dealings. While there, he often heard local gossip about Gloyd's drinking, which he immediately brought home to his daughter. Yet Carry's faith was unshakable, and she told Gloyd as well as her parents that nothing would prevent her marriage to him once she was twenty-one. Since that date was rapidly approaching, George may have decided that if he gave his consent one less strain would be placed upon the young couple. Reluctantly, George and Mary agreed to the marriage. The wedding ceremony was to take place in the Cass County House on November 21, 1867, four days before Carry's twenty-first birthday.

The morning dawned ominously for such a happy event. Low, heavy mist hung over the Missouri hills, and the bare, skeletonlike trees dripped moisture. Gloyd arrived in a fancy rig, but Carry noticed his eyes were strangely glazed. During the wedding ceremony he mumbled the words and his speech was slurred.

For the first time, Carry saw that Charles Gloyd was thoroughly intoxicated.

CHAPTER 4

After the wedding, Carry's battered old trunk was bound to Gloyd's buggy and they set out for Holden. The trip was a strained one, as would be the marriage. Charles Gloyd, a bit more sober than when he had arrived, was bringing his wife home for a honeymoon in the small house where his mother and father lived. Carry, more uneasy than disillusioned, wondered if she had done the right thing in breaking with her loving father for a husband who could face this special day only under the influence of alcohol.

Charles Gloyd had become an alcoholic while in the army. In his youth, he had been an excellent medical student, who was a sensitive loner and an avid reader. When the Civil War broke out, he was given the rank of captain in the 118th Regiment of the Union Army, and he soon discovered that drinking would relax him in social situations with his fellow officers. Sober, he was withdrawn and felt uncomfortable in friendly gatherings, but under the effect of alcohol, he became a lively, humorous companion. Soon he was a steady, compulsive drinker.

CARRY NATION

Five days after the wedding, Gloyd did not arrive home for supper. This was the first such episode, so Carry's thoughts ran to terrifying images of injury and accidents. Late that night, Gloyd staggered into the house and headed for his bedroom without even speaking to his wife. Collapsing onto his bed, he fell into a deep sleep.

His mother entered the room, leaned over his inert form, and then straightened quickly. When Mother Gloyd left the room, shaking her head, Carry bent over to examine her husband's face. The sickening odor of liquor assailed her nostrils.

The next day Gloyd promised never to take another drink. He went to his medical office, but did not return until after midnight, his footsteps unsteady, his words slurred. Night after night he repeated the same drunken routine, and night after night he assured Carry, who had waited by the front window for him, that this was the very last time he would have a drink. The sober promise was always suffocated by the fumes of alcohol. Yet, reportedly, he told her, "Pet, I'd give my right arm to make you happy."

Gloyd's parents were no help to Carry in her efforts to combat his drinking, and the presence of at least one of them may have been a major cause of Charles's alcoholism. His father was a fine gentleman—bedridden, but always able to maintain a peppery air. Mother Gloyd, however, was a resolute New Englander, self-sufficient, set in her ways, and extremely puritanical. Whenever she was around, Charles became silent and standoffish even toward Carry, and tended to smoke heavily, another sin in Carry's former home. Escape for Gloyd came only through drink, and his favorite haunt was the Masonic Lodge.

One night Carry became so overwrought that she

42

threw her shawl around her shoulders and set off for the local drinking spot, but pounding on the front door of the Lodge brought her only a reprimand that women were not allowed on the premises. Carry then found the back door and hammered loudly at it, upsetting the drunken conviviality inside with anguished cries that her husband be released.

Her nightly attacks on this bastion of masculinity continued for months, even after she had become pregnant. In church, too, her demands upon the preacher and the congregation for special prayers to help her errant husband interrupted the services continually. If Carry was shopping and spied a Mason on the street, she collared the individual, making it seem his personal fault that Charles Gloyd was an alcoholic.

Though her cause was just, her methods managed to alienate even her friends, who began avoiding Carry. Throughout Holden, she gained a reputation for being a hysterical crank, which was linked with the assumption that her actions had driven Gloyd to liquor rather than the reverse. Instead of sympathy and help, she received ridicule and became the town joke.

Gloyd's reputation for heavy drinking frightened his patients so that his practice fell off sharply. Money became scarce in the Gloyd household—money for food and rent, that is; Charles always seemed to have enough cash for his nightly binges.

Another fear befell Carry, and it concerned their unborn child. She remembered that the Bible told how the mother of Samson was warned by an angel to drink neither wine nor strong drink before her child was born, or the result would be a weakened infant. Carry now worried that her husband's carousing might already have inflicted harm upon the unborn baby.

Meanwhile, George Moore, who had business connections in Holden, heard that Carry was practically penniless, pregnant, and had a husband who was drunk more often than he was sober. In midsummer of 1868, Moore arrived at the Gloyd home in Holden and was shocked at his daughter's physical and mental state when she threw herself into his arms, weeping. Frightened that Carry might fall prey to her mother's mental illness, Moore packed Carry's bag while she waited in the wagon. Then he took her back to Belton.

The marriage was finished, though at the time Carry did not know it, for hope still lingered in her heart. She wrote to Charles every day, pleading with him to take a pledge to stop drinking. Carry explained repeatedly that the reason she had returned home was not a lack of love for him but the dreadful effect alcohol was having on their marriage and happiness. In his replies Charles begged her to return. He declared that only with her by his side would he be able to stop drinking. Carry wanted to believe Charles, but too many similar promises had been broken. Now she must think of their child.

Carry was to see Gloyd only once again. In September 1868, a daughter was born to her: Charlien. Six weeks later, Mary let Carry and her brother go to Holden to collect the remainder of Carry's belongings. Her mother warned Carry that if she stayed in Holden, she would never be allowed to come home again. The warning was needless, because Carry's own common sense dictated that she could never remain with Charles as long as he drank so heavily. Her love had not died; she was only being realistic about the state of their marriage.

When Carry met Charles, he was full of promises to stop drinking, but his breath reeked of liquor. Carry later wrote, "I saw I could not depend upon my husband though at that time I did not know that drinking men were drugged men, diseased men." She instructed her brother to bind her old trunk to the buggy for its return trip to Belton.

In a final attempt to stop Carry, Gloyd grabbed her arm. "If you leave me, I'll be a dead man inside six months." It was the alcoholic's customary attempt to place the blame on another.

Forcibly, Carry pulled herself free and climbed into the wagon. She nodded to her brother, and the buggy rolled homeward.

Even in his alcohol-fuzzed brain, Gloyd knew the parting was final, and he consoled himself by drinking even more. When his father died four months later, all restraints seemed broken, and Charles was hardly able to claim a sober hour. Six months from the day of the birth of Charlien, the daughter he never saw, Gloyd died of acute and chronic alcoholism.

When Carry received the telegram about his death, Gloyd's last words echoed in her mind: *If you leave me, I'll be a dead man inside six months.* Her lifelong tendency to claim guilt as solely her own took control. Carry collapsed and was bedridden for days, while she constantly mulled over what might have happened if she had stayed with her husband. Would he have stopped drinking? Carry didn't know. But now she would never know. Desperately, she sought means for making amends for what she considered *her* sins.

Realizing that Mother Gloyd was living alone and had no money or source of income, Carry decided that one way to atone to Charles would be to care for his mother. Despite her own parents' objections, Carry packed her belongings, placed Charlien in the buggy, and prepared to return to Holden.

As Carry rode away that day, her trunk now making

its third trip between Holden and Belton, she did not know what lay before her. Certainly she didn't realize that she would not see the family farm again until both her parents were dead and her brothers and sisters were living in far parts of the country. Nor did she comprehend that the only way she could exorcise her overwhelming though unjustified remorse would be to place the blame squarely on that which had destroyed Charles: alcohol. At this point, she only wished to help Mother Gloyd and Charlien.

Immediately, she sold Gloyd's medical instruments and textbooks as well as several sections of land her father had given her. She retained one lot on which she built a compact, three-room house. When she, Charlien, and Mother Gloyd had moved into the smaller residence, she then rented out the Gloyd home. The rent was only a small income, so Carry knew she needed other means to sustain the household. She applied to and was accepted at Warrensburg Normal Institute. Leaving Charlien with her mother-in-law, Carry went to begin her preparation for a teaching career.

While in Warrensburg, Carry was attending the Christian Church one Sunday when a tall man, David A. Nation, took the pulpit and preached the day's sermon. Nation, who was a part-time preacher and also acting editor of the Warrensburg *Journal,* was considered by all to be a distinguished citizen of the community. He was fiercely domineering with his full beard and his dark, probing eyes, which some people described as burning with intelligence and others labeled self-righteousness. However, neither that day's message nor the man himself made much of an impression on Carry, who was still suffering from guilt, but years later she would remember this particular Sunday as something out of the ordinary, possibly an omen.

Upon graduating, Carry secured a position as a primary teacher in the Holden public school. After the long period of hardship, life seemed to have righted itself. Her salary plus the small rental income were enough to support the family of three. Understandably, Carry felt proud that she had called upon her own inner resources and eased what had been a nasty situation.

Months passed and then years, four in all, and then, one day, a member of the school board visited Carry's classroom. The man, who was secretly seeking a teaching position for his niece, criticized Carry's reading lesson, in which she was instructing the pupils to pronounce the letter *a* with the Midwestern sound rather than the New England long *a* sound.

Carry, her stubbornness aroused by the nonsensical criticism, informed the board member that the children should learn to speak the way people talked in Missouri. After all, she told him, the school was in Holden, not Boston.

The board member, who was both inflated with self-importance and hiding an ulterior motive, promptly had Carry fired.

Though her stubborn pride had not let her give in to the foolish man, the prospect of no job was a serious problem for Carry. A new teaching position would mean leaving Mother Gloyd and Charlien and going to another town. This thought was depressing. But what else was there to do?

Suddenly, as Carry later told the story, the solution came on the wings of inspiration. Marriage.

Carry prayed for assistance. "My Lord, you see the

situation. I can't take care of Mother and Charlien. I want You to help me. I have no one picked out, but won't You select the one You think best. I want to give You my life. I want, by marrying, to glorify You and serve You as well as take care of Mother and Charlien and be a good wife."

Carry was nearly thirty, but she was not without attractive qualities at this time. Her height was still her most impressive attribute, six feet, and she had intense dark eyes. Her face had become rather rounded, but her mouth remained straight and full, while her chin jutted out defiantly as if daring life to strike another blow. Unfortunately, she did not have long to wait.

A week after her prayer session, she was walking down the main street of Holden when she spotted an impressive-looking gentleman standing in a doorway. He turned and lifted his hat, smiling. In that moment, Carry experienced "a peculiar thrill." The man, David A. Nation, sent her a note the next day, requesting that they enter into correspondence. To Carry, it seemed as if God had answered her prayers.

Others were doubtful about the divine influence on this match. Mother Gloyd and Carry's friends insisted that Nation was too old for her—he was nineteen years her senior and a widower with an eight-year-old daughter. But, as always, Carry wanted what she wanted and would brook no one's interference. In 1877, Carry Amelia Gloyd, thirty years old, wed David A. Nation. The only thing the couple had in common was the same middle initial.

After renting the Holden house, Carry, Charlien, and Mother Gloyd moved into Warrensburg with Nation and his daughter Lola. From the beginning there was trouble because of the simple fact that Carry and David were sharply different personalities who had married for convenience rather than love. Carry was young and vital and was still approaching the peak of her ambitions, though at this moment she was not aware in which direction her goal lay. David Nation's life had crested and he was beginning to reach the point where he could only look back on his achievements. The Nations had small arguments, never anything major or violent, just a steady, nagging hostile relationship.

"My combative nature was largely developed by living with him," Carry later said. "For I had to fight for everything I had."

For that matter, David too had reached a point where life was a constant struggle. First, he lost his job at the Warrensburg *Journal*, and next, at about the same time, he learned there were no openings for a preacher. Though Nation was a licensed lawyer, practice in Warrensburg was a closed occupation, limited to a few local families.

Deciding that farming might be the answer, the Nations bought a seventeen-hundred-acre farm on the San Bernard River in southern Texas. For Carry, the whole experience must have been reminiscent of her father's ill-fated venture in Grayson County. The Nations invested much of their capital in fine herds of cattle, horses, and pigs, but as had happened with her father, eight of the Nation's nine horses died that spring, and the remainder of the stock slowly perished afterward. They managed to get the cotton crop planted in time, but soon after that, David picked a quarrel with a neighbor, who sought revenge by throwing the Nations' plow and tools into the river. Another of David's errors in judgment occurred the day he hired a farmhand who later absconded with all the cash he could find in the house.

At this moment, with his life sliding downhill, Nation optimistically hoped to halt the fall by setting up a law practice in Brazoria, Texas. He packed his bags, leaving Carry and Mother Gloyd and the two girls to tend the farm. Remarkably, Carry harvested the cotton fields, now gone mostly to weed, and sold the crop for a low price. Any money was most welcome, for there was no milk, bread, or butter. The family's daily diet consisted mainly of sweet potatoes, corn meal, and bacon fat. Sickness was common because of the inadequate food supply.

While the family was literally existing at the starvation level, a letter arrived from David. Could they send him money because his plans for a law practice had not succeeded?

The marriage that was supposed to bring her family security and happiness had dragged Carry to her lowest point of desperation. Again, she sought help from the only source available to her. She prayed.

CHAPTER 5

The answer came from nearby Columbia, a terminus for the Columbia Tap Railroad, when the owner of the Columbia Hotel offered to let Carry run his establishment. The town's population at that time hovered around five hundred people, so the business opportunities were not great. Carry had one thing in her favor, however: Mother Gloyd had once been an innkeeper in New England. Unhesitatingly, Carry packed up the family and all their belongings and moved into Columbia.

The dilapidated hotel would have disheartened anyone who lacked Carry's determination, but she borrowed $3.50 from the husband of her cook and set about trying to make the building livable. Newspapers and old cloth were pasted over the holes in the plaster walls. Essential windowpanes were replaced. Old sheets were converted into curtains. And the structure was thoroughly fumigated in a grim effort to destroy rats and bedbugs. When the first few tenants registered, the rent money was instantly rushed to the grocery store to buy the evening's meal.

David Nation's role in running the hotel was ambiguous, though his part seems mostly to have been designed to charm the guests. At times he acted as a well-dressed desk clerk, but at other times he escaped and wandered about Columbia, still trying to establish a law practice. Each night, without fail, however, he sat with the hotel tenants, ate the well-prepared meals, and entertained everyone with his conversation. Carry and the family lived on scraps.

The workday for Carry was long and strenuous. She would rise an hour before dawn, help the cook, serve in the dining room, and then wash and iron the tablecloths. Soon she added the boarders' laundry to her chores, and her work hours stretched till after midnight. With a seven-day week and approximately four hours sleep each night, the routine began to exact its toll.

Nervousness gave way to insomnia, and that led to spells of depression and hysterical fits. Night after night, though her body was racked with exhaustion, she could not sleep. Then the mature Carry found a solace that had once helped the young Carry—a solitary spot from which she could gaze out at the world and think. Now her hidden ledge was a tiny hotel room, and her view of the world consisted of a saloon across the street. Sitting there and brooding, she wondered how different her life might now be if Gloyd had not become trapped by alcoholism. As she thought, the real villain slowly became clear to her, and a growing need to do something about this enemy, alcohol, awakened within her.

Unfortunately, her memory, always sharp and sound, began to falter. Often a passerby would meet Carry on the street, and Carry could remember neither her own name nor her reason for being out. Other times, spells of frenetic praying would seize her. "Her supplicating cries could be heard a block away," one reporter wrote, and the man claimed the hotel seemed to "tremble" as Carry moved about her room, advancing on her knees, as she had learned to do years before at boarding school.

If sleep did come for a few fitful hours, so did terrible nightmares. She suffered from a recurring dream in which two snakes appeared. One was large and fat; the other, scrawny. The larger snake would strike at Carry in her dream, hissing as she tried to flee. Frequently, she woke up screaming. Then, after a night of little sleep and dreadful nightmares, Carry had to face another day of toil from dawn until midnight.

The times were bleak. "I began to see how little there was in life. I wondered at the gaiety of people. It seemed a pall hung over the earth. I would wonder that the birds sung, or the sun would shine."

Still, she maintained her vigil during those small hours of the morning when she could not, or feared to, sleep, and gazed at the saloon across the street. Seeing late-evening customers leave the establishment with unsteady footsteps, Carry wondered if their loyal wives waited at home, hoping and crying. An unshakable conviction gripped Carry that the curse upon herself and on all these unhappy families was, indeed, alcohol.

As if her work load and emotional burdens were not enough, another worry came. For the last few years Carry had been concerned that Charlien had at first ignored and then openly ridiculed religion, and would have nothing to do with church or with the Bible. If Carry insisted that Charlien attend services, the girl would have a wild tantrum and have to be locked in her room. Carry was terrified that Charlien might become an atheist. Remembering the tales of eternal damnation told by the slaves, Carry prayed for God to punish her daughter with some bodily affliction that would also cause Charlien to respect and love God. Immediately, Carry regretted this action, for she knew there must be a way to bring the girl to the Lord through love.

Soon after, however, Charlien grew pale and began wasting away, while at the same time her fits of temper increased in frequency. Thus weakened, Charlien developed typhoid fever. Day and night, Carry nursed her, taking as much time from her duties as she dared. When the girl began to recover, her right cheek became badly swollen. Upon investigation, Carry discovered a large ulcerating sore eating through Charlien's cheek. Despite applications of internal and external remedies, the cheek fell out, horribly exposing Charlien's teeth.

Hotel residents and personal friends claimed that the doctor's administrations had been at fault, but Carry remembered her fervent prayer of a month before. Thus, she claimed more personal guilt in her own mind. Determined that Charlien should not perish, Carry sat by her bedside for nine long days. A minister advised her that it would be better for the child to die, because if Charlien lived, her face would be dreadfully deformed. Carry did not agree, and she held her post.

Whether it was Carry's intense faith or her granite-hard willpower, the sore, which has had no known similarities in medical history, slowly began to heal. After ten days the hole had shrunk to the size of a quarter. But just when Charlien seemed on the brink of recovery, a new problem arose. Her jaws clamped shut as if she were suffering from tetanus and would not open. In order for the girl to be fed, several of her front teeth had to be knocked out and a metal tube inserted into her mouth. The constant fear now was that Charlien might strangle.

Then Carry began to remember Charles Gloyd's impressive intake of liquor just before she became pregnant with Charlien. The belief that she was the direct cause of the girl's health problems began to disappear as she shifted the blame onto her foe, alcohol. Again she read the biblical warning about strong drink while carrying a child. She became aware, too, of another sign that Gloyd's drinking had harmed the unborn child. Along with her physical weakness, Charlien was dull-witted. Today her intelligence would be rated as subnormal.

"The curse of heredity is one of the most heartbreaking results of the saloon," Carry later wrote.

Another mark had been checked against liquor.

A bright spot in these dark times was the sale of the cotton farm on the San Bernard River. Carry used this income to bring Charlien to Dr. Dowell in Galveston. Four operations were required to close the hole in Charlien's cheek completely, but the surgeon found no way to open her locked jaws. More years and the help of medical specialists from San Antonio to Philadelphia were needed before plastic surgery had hidden the scar on Charlien's cheek and her jaws began to operate normally once again. The process was a physical and psychological strain on Charlien, for at times forcible prying had been employed, resulting in great pain. But at last came the day when Charlien arrived home, seemingly recovered from her harrowing experiences.

During this same time period, Carry learned of a hotel for sale in Richmond, a town near Houston. Investigating the property, Carry found the hotel to consist of twenty rooms with six cottages; a sizable improvement over the Columbia Hotel. In 1881, Carry took an option on the property.

While Carry was in the midst of hotel negotiations,

her father visited her, but he would not live permanently with the Nations. First, Mary's condition had become more complicated and she was having wilder tantrums and bouts of incoherent shrieking. A hotel would not be a fitting place for her. Also, the Richmond hotel was an old, wooden structure, a potential fire trap. Carry, who had had a dread of fire since the days the slaves had spoken of the vengeful flames of hell, would often awaken at night, believing she smelled smoke. She would then roam the hotel from floor to floor, seeking the cause. So she knew that someone would have to be in her mother's company constantly to prevent a tragedy. Reluctantly, Carry had to bid good-bye to her father.

At their parting, George Moore told her, "I've always hoped to have something to leave you, and it's such a grief to me I can't help you."

"You've left me something far better."

"What is that?" asked George.

"The memory of a father who never did a dishonorable act."

Carry was never to see her father again. When he died in Missouri shortly after, she could not leave the hotel to attend his funeral. She did scrape together enough cash to pay his last debts of a few hundred dollars. By doing this, she prayed that he might rest more peacefully. After George's death, Mary was committed to the Missouri State Hospital for the Insane at Nevada, Missouri.

For Carry, the new hotel meant even more work to meet the mortgage payments. Also the list of people she had to support was growing. Mother Gloyd, David Nation, and Charlien shared at least part of Carry's burden, but Nation's daughter, Lola, had married William Riddle and brought him to live in the hotel, too. Besides more family members, there were a greater number of guests, so that additional meals had to be served and there was more laundry to be washed and ironed. Carry began to wonder if she would ever escape from the mire of financial obligations.

In spite of her tremendous work load, Carry did find time to continue her spiritual mission. The Methodists and the Episcopalians refused to admit her to their churches. The former claimed she was "too religious," and the latter were disturbed when she insisted the church catachism be discarded. Carry, therefore, started her own nondenominational Sunday school, which met in the hotel dining room. She also collected food and clothing and prepared baskets for the needy in Richmond.

One day a painfully thin young man knocked on the kitchen door, seeking odd jobs as a tin repairman. Carry subsequently learned that the fellow was suffering from tuberculosis. At her own expense, even though money was scarce, she sent him to a New York sanatorium. Years later, recovered, the man set up a tourist booth near Niagara Falls and became a successful businessman. He never forgot Carry. He wrote to her that during his illness he had seen no use for religion, but that he had become a devout Christian. This alone repaid Carry more than money.

The only dark cloud in terms of religion was Charlien, who still would not attend church or have anything to do with Carry's Sunday school. Yet Charlien, now married to Alexander McNab, who was also living in the hotel, was to be the catalyst for one of the two remarkable happenings Carry experienced in Texas. These occurrences were described in Carry's autobiography but were also fully documented by objective witnesses.

CARRY NATION

A drought had settled over Richmond and the surrounding lands, killing the cotton crop and drying up water supplies for livestock. The farmers of Fort Bend County were desperate, and feared they could not avoid financial ruin. Store owners, too, faced bankruptcy. One day Charlien told Carry that she ought to pray for rain because God listened to her. Even this small indication of faith was enough to propel Carry into action. She convinced the Methodist church officials to allow her to use the church basement for a meeting to "offer supplications for additional moisture."

A few people eagerly agreed to attend; others were hesitant. The minister's wife wept, saying, "I have read of so many thunderbolts lately that I am almost afraid to pray."

Carry was adamant, however, and collected a small band of followers. The county paper later described the afternoon convocation. "She (Carry) had a style not usually noticed in entreaties before the Lord; agressive, not humble, her eyes wide open for one thing, and her bonnetted head waggling back and forth as though she'd lost patience with everybody in the Celestial Organization."

The session was an exhausting one for Carry, who actively led the hours-long effort to bring rain. "After the meeting we were standing on the platform in front of the church when a sprinkle of rain out of a cloudless sky fell on the platform and the shutters of the house. This was nothing but a miracle and was very astonishing to us all. The next day clouds began to gather in the sky and the moisture started, at first, to come down in the gentlest manner and continued in this way for three days."

Many residents of Richmond took notice; others scoffed and insisted that the area would have had rain with or without Carry's prayers. However, the disbelievers were to face another inexplicable event, and this time they would be even more hard pressed to voice their disclaimers.

If water was involved in the first strange episode, it was fire the next time.

In March 1889, Carry was summoned late one night by an elderly guest who was suffering painful stomach cramps. Tending to her tenants' minor health complaints was another of Carry's numerous duties, so she went to the kitchen and heated a mustard plaster, which she applied to the man's stomach. As Carry climbed the cold stairway back to her own room, ". . . there seemed to be a light shining behind me, which would come and go in flashes, as I ascended. I looked everywhere to see where it came from but discovered it had to be an unnatural manifestation." Again she mounted the creaky wooden steps, and again the pulsating golden glow seemed to follow her. This time she understood and did not fear the unearthly glow, for it was "the sweet presence of God."

The next morning, Carry spoke of the vision and warned her family to expect trouble.

That night, at precisely the same hour she had seen the mysterious light the previous night, Carry was awakened by Charlien's screams. "Wake up, Mama! The whole town is on fire!"

In the early morning hours, a fire had started in a drugstore and was now raging through most of the business district.

The hotel guests were immediately roused and told to flee. People scrambled down the halls and stairs in their nightclothes, carrying what few belongings they could gather into their arms.

In nightgown and robe, Carry knelt and prayed. "Oh, God, you told me to call on you in a day of trouble! This is my day of trouble!"

Bucket brigades were organized in the streets, but the fire had gained too much headway. The air was filled with acrid smoke and the crackling and crashing sounds of collapsing buildings. Inside the hotel, confusion reigned. A long-time boarder was directing two blacks to carry out her elegant furniture. Seeing Carry on her knees, she urged Carry to get up and save some of the hotel's valuables. Carry continued to pray.

"The poor woman's lost her mind," decided the lady.

Other guests were also trying to save the hotel's furnishings. A man grabbed an expensive red plush chair and prepared to drag the piece of furniture to safety.

"Let it be!" shouted Carry.

The man halted, amazed. "Are you insured?"

"Yes, up there." Carry pointed to heaven.

As Carry calmly walked into the hotel parlor, sat down in a rocking chair, and began praying, the other guests knew they had no time left to argue. The moment had come when they must save themselves. Running outside, they saw the red and yellow flames hopscotching down the street. The conflagration was three buildings away, then two, and soon the tinderbox next to the hotel erupted into fierce flames.

Above the fire's roar everyone heard Carry's raucous voice singing hymns from a psalmbook while certain death bore down upon her.

And then a miracle happened.

The wind suddenly shifted, and the fire's progress slowed, halted. The building next to the fire-trap hotel slowly burned into a smoldering pile of charred beams and white ashes.

People rushed into the hotel, telling Carry, "You're safe."

Her response was a confident smile, for Carry had never doubted the eventual outcome. Later, she wrote, "From that day to this, I have never had any fear of fire."

The two incidents, however, were to have a more profound effect upon Carry's life besides erasing a long-time fear of fire. Two strands were slowly converging in her mind. One belief, strengthened by the two happenings in Richmond, was that there was a divine influence upon her life and, in effect, a direct connection between heavenly wishes and the direction her path must lead. Her other belief was the firm conviction that her worst enemy on this earth was alcohol. When these two threads became intertwined, their strength would be so great that even the President of the United States would have to contend with Carry Nation.

The moment was drawing nearer by the day.

CHAPTER 6

It is not unusual for what appears to be a negative event in a person's life to be recognized years later as the step that led the individual toward an unexpected destiny. So it was with Carry Nation. As her fame spread through Fort Bend County, her hotel business became more prosperous. Although more tenants meant a heavier work schedule, at least the constant worry of meeting the mortgage payments was eased by the money flowing into the hotel coffers. In fact, Carry could even envision a bright future when she would one day own the property. And, then, as was symptomatic of her life, another move became necessary.

The Texas town was experiencing what most Southern states would endure for the next one hundred years. The Civil War was over, and the basic human freedoms had been legally granted to the blacks. Regrettably, these rights were not always recognized. Richmond boasted two warring factions who were divided on this controversial racist issue: the Peckerwoods and the Jaybirds. The Peckerwoods, of which David Nation was a member, insisted the blacks be allowed to vote and hold

62

office. Bitter opposition came from the Jaybirds, who were mostly teenage hoodlums.

David Nation, a part-time correspondent for the Houston *Post*, wrote an article condemning the Jaybirds as a gang of rowdies who used the issue of white supremacy as an excuse for hooliganism. The newspaper piece described how the Jaybirds ran rampant along the streets of Richmond late at night, disturbing the peace and committing acts of vandalism.

As was his custom, David Nation always met the midnight train in Richmond. One night as Nation waited, Henry George, a Jaybird, said he wanted to talk to him, and he led David toward a huge bale of cotton. A gang of young punks attacked Nation with canes and clubs.

When David staggered back to the hotel, Carry bathed his battered face and bruised body in cold water and applied soothing medications. While Nation was laid up for the next few days, the Jaybirds decreed that no Peckerwoods would be allowed to remain in Richmond. Soon after, a Western-style shoot-out erupted in which the sheriff of Richmond was killed.

Immediately, the whole town armed itself in preparation for open warfare. Those who dared to walk the streets at night kept their hands close to their gun handles. One night an unknown sniper shot at David. Although Nation escaped injury, he and Carry knew they must leave Texas. David, who had accepted a position as pastor of the First Christian Church in Medicine Lodge, Kansas, departed first. A few weeks were needed for Carry to complete the final arrangements of a business deal in which she exchanged the Richmond hotel for a house in Medicine Lodge.

Though she had experienced many uprootings

since the age of nine, Carry found this to be one of the most traumatic, because her family of many years was being scattered. Lola and Charlien and their husbands had to find homes elsewhere, but the separation that was most grievous to Carry was leaving Mother Gloyd until enough money could be raised to bring the old woman to Kansas. Two of Carry's friends volunteered to take the eighty-six-year-old woman into their homes and care for her. But Mother Gloyd could not bear to part from Carry.

"You'll be better off here in Richmond," Carry told her. "Kansas is much colder."

"I was born in Vermont, and it's very cold there," argued Mother Gloyd.

The old woman continued to press the issue, pleading with Carry to allow her to come to Kansas immediately rather than at some indefinite date in the future. Carry might have weakened, but David had given strict orders that the family budget could not support one more person. The morning Carry went to the railroad station, Mother Gloyd appeared there with her packed trunk and clung to Carry desperately.

"I have lived with you for twenty-three years, and I want to die with you. Not alone." Weeping, Mother Gloyd was led away by friends.

To Carry, it must have seemed to be all happening once again. Another Gloyd begging not to be separated from her, another Gloyd declaring a lonely death would be the result. Steeling her defenses as much as she could, Carry boarded the train for the long, hot journey to Kansas, but the guilty memory of her first husband was a fellow passenger.

There is a story, which may be apocryphal, that Carry returned to Richmond years later and was shown the graves of the Jaybirds who had driven her family from town. Reportedly, Carry reveled in the news that the men had met early and violent deaths. As she stood at their graves, she is said to have raised a clenched right fist to heaven, declaring, "Vengeance is mine; I will repay."

But now she was heading toward Medicine Lodge, Kansas, a small, dusty town deep in the cyclone belt of the Midwest. In the sixteenth century, the Spanish explorer Coronado had traveled along the Medicine River, but his band had found nothing appealing about its dry, parched shores. Medicine Lodge had had a moment of glory during the 1870's and early 1880's as Easterners, seeking lives as cattlemen and farmers, moved west and settled on the riverbanks, but the town's economy had peaked quickly and was already tumbling downward again when Carry arrived in 1893.

For the first six months that the Nations were in Medicine Lodge, they lived in a boardinghouse until their new home was vacated by its previous owners. To the forty-six-year-old Carry this was a sudden and, at first, pleasant change from the rigorous routine of running a hotel. Relaxed for the first time in years, she slipped into the role of pastor's wife and attended Sunday services at the First Christian Church.

Discontent began to surface, however, when Carry observed David, week after week, delivering what she viewed as flabby sermons. Taking it upon herself, she began to edit his texts and then coauthor them by inserting attacks against tobacco, sex, and liquor. At times the actual names of church members were mentioned as those individuals Carry knew were yielding to temptation.

Even worse for her reputation, Carry sat in the front

pew each Sunday and told David what to do, as if she were a theatrical director. In a voice that, unfortuntately, could be heard throughout the building, she would urge him to speak louder or softer, to walk to the right, and to point to heaven. When she felt his sermon had gone on long enough, she would say loudly, "That will be all for today, David," and then she would march to the pulpit and slam shut his Bible.

Her Sunday performances acquired a negative fame, and soon each week the small church was packed by people who were more interested in Carry than in the spiritual message. Though she did not realize the fact at the time, this effort to guide David along certain lines was a psychological attempt, in effect, to place herself in front of the congregation. Many of the gestures and mannerisms she imposed upon David would soon be duplicated in her own public appearances.

Adding to her image of town eccentric was her obsession with illicit sex. Walking along Main Street, Kansas Avenue, or First Avenue, she stopped young couples and asked them, "Do you believe in God?" No matter what their answer was, she would then launch into a lecture concerning the evils of sex. Nightly, she prowled the dark lanes and alleys of Medicine Lodge, carrying a wicked-looking umbrella, which had a sharpened ferrule.

"As I was going down to a neighbor's one dark night," she later wrote, "I heard low voices of persons sitting by the roadside. I got a lantern." Armed with the light and the umbrella, she confronted a young couple. "You should act toward this girl as you would toward your sister," she told the boy. Carry warned the girl, "Ruin will be your fate if you keep on this way."

Reportedly, the young man and woman fled down

the road to escape Carry. In fact, many people in Kansas town went in the opposite direction whenever they saw Carry—night or day.

Carry, however, also won admirers due to her unrelenting efforts to aid the poor and needy. At Thanksgiving and Christmas, she packed her buggy with food and gifts and made a circuit of the many homes where these free donations were welcomed. On one occasion she learned of a new family named French who had just moved into a small house three miles outside of town. Arriving with baskets of food, Carry helped Mrs. French feed the large family their first nourishing meal in weeks. Mrs. French was so grateful that she wept. "It takes so little to make some people happy," Carry told her friends.

Her activities inspired others. C. O. Chandler, a wealthy man in Medicine Lodge, allowed Carry to bring poor children to his home, where they were fed, and he told her to buy clothing and fuel for destitute families at his expense.

Mother Nation was the name given to Carry by the recipients of these badly needed gifts, but future events were to make the name an uncomfortable reminder for Carry.

Life was not going smoothly for the Nations. David learned that he would not be reappointed as pastor and began searching for another position. Faced with this insecurity, Carry received additional bad news. On September 24, 1893, her mother died in the Missouri State Hospital at Nevada. Though relations between Carry and Mary had never been smooth, Carry brooded about her mother's death. For one thing Carry had a fear of institutions. For another she believed that if she had taken her mother from the hospital and cared for her, she might have lived a few years longer.

Then, before Carry could adjust to this self-accusation, she received word from Texas that Mother Gloyd was seriously ill. Carry wanted to return to Richmond immediately, but the Nations could not afford the money. Three days later, Mrs. Gloyd died.

Guilt plagued Carry, who had always been strongly affected by death. Charles had prophesied he would die if she deserted him, and he had. Mother Gloyd had begged not to be allowed to die alone. And Mary Moore had spent her last moments in a tiny, cell-like room. Carry felt as if she herself had in some way caused all these sad, lonely deaths.

Before Carry could subdue her personal demons, David was given a position as minister in Holton, Kansas, and once more Carry packed all their belongings. The Medicine Lodge home was rented, and the Nations moved to northeast Kansas. The stay was short because David's job lasted only a few months. Carry and David then returned to Medicine Lodge, where David hoped to set up a law practice.

This unsettled existence, plus her sorrow over the recent deaths of her mother and Mother Gloyd, drove Carry into spells of remorse. As before, she sought solace in religion. Carry applied for sainthood at the two local churches, but her requests were denied. The official reason was that the churches wanted proof of the two experiences in Richmond where Carry had apparently ended a drought and had had a vision of the town fire. The probable reason for the refusal was that many churchgoers considered Carry a nuisance. Though she was at times sensitive and shy, Carry from her youngest years had always wanted to be the center of attraction.

Therefore, when she attended church, she would interrupt the services to present her own sermons or demand that certain hymns be sung. If her requests were ignored, she snatched the hymnals from the members of the congregation until they agreed to sing the music she had selected. Despite these actions, Carry was able to befriend some church officials in Medicine Lodge.

One stormy night, the Baptist minister, the Reverend Laurence Cain, and his daughter visited the Nations. Carry played the organ and the small group sang hymns, read the Bible, and prayed.

Suddenly, in the flashes of lightning outside, Carry saw and heard wings beating at the window. "Something was poured on my head, running all over and through me, which I call divine electricity." She rushed into the pouring rain, knocked on neighbors' doors, and called upon them to lift their voices in prayer because God had bestowed a "divine gift" upon her.

Returning home, she immediately went to the basement and read the Bible, finding "every word and every letter" surrounded by "a bright light." Even the interpretation of the most obscure passages, which had previously eluded her, was now a simple matter.

For the next three days and nights, without food or sleep, Carry remained in the basement reading the Bible. At times she would be possessed by periods of visions and prayer. She saw the earth split apart by jagged streaks of lightning while she and Jesus stood safe in a circle of heavenly light. At other times she would sing hymns and pray, advancing upon her knees. She emerged from this experience certain in her knowledge that she had been appointed by God for a mission on earth, and that this mission would be focused against her long-time enemy, alcohol.

Carry, at last, had found a target for all the self-assumed guilts and troubles that had emotionally persecuted her. If alcohol had been responsible for so much wrong, then she could not be at fault. And the more vehemently she attacked what she viewed as the evils in the world, the more she would cleanse her own conscience.

Now that her personal recriminations had at last been stilled, Carry emerged from her three-day session a changed person. A quiet determination and an almost supreme self-confidence marked her manner, and would continue to do so for the rest of her life except for a few brief periods.

At the age of fifty-three, Carry, a solitary crusader, was about to do battle with one of the largest economic forces of the time: the liquor industry.

CHAPTER 7

Today people sometimes underestimate the political and economic power wielded in the late nineteenth century by those engaged in the liquor traffic. Alcohol was the Big Business of the day, equivalent to contemporary industrial corporations. In Carry's time, citizens still remembered the scandals of the "Whiskey Ring," which had weakened the already corrupt administration of President Grant. Members of the government, including Grant's personal secretary, schemed to defraud the government of millions of dollars in federal taxes on liquor.

From the earliest Colonial times, rum was a main staple of American trade and an important component of daily life. It was not uncommon for mothers to feed their crying infants alcohol to still them. Clergymen in the East often owned interests in distilleries and taverns; some even tended bar in their off-hours. In the early 1800's there were reports of twelve-year-old children thoroughly intoxicated on street corners in Albany, New York. As for the Midwest, Dr. Karl Menninger, a founder of the Menninger Clinic in Topeka, described Kansas during his grandmother's lifetime, which was the same period that Carry was embarking upon her crusade.

Drunken marauding was a pretty serious thing in those days [Menninger said]. One must remember that the state [Kansas] was full of psychopaths and unstable characters who had failed in the East and had come out here to make a new start. They caused a lot more damage to life and property than did the Indians. It was tough going out here and the temptation to get drunk and forget it was pretty widespread.

Kansas was also the state that in 1880—the year Carry was operating the run-down hotel in Columbia, Texas—had specified that liquor could be sold only for "medical, scientific and mechanical" purposes. The result was that "joints," or illegal bars, flourished, with the owners, or "jointists," paying fines, which were more like blackmail payoffs, to law-enforcement officers who periodically arrested them. Once the fine had been handed over, the joint would reopen until the next payment was due. A bar even operated near the state capitol and was openly frequented by some of the same legislators who had approved the 1880 law. In addition, drugstores sold tremendous quantities of alcohol. Some establishments simply set up a plank bar, whereas other druggists required doctors' notes, which explained that the customer could buy liquor with the "refillable prescription for chronic alcoholism."

Therefore, Carry's foe was not an imaginary one, and it was an opponent that viewed her initial efforts as mere insect bites, unworthy of any notice other than a quick brush-off. With her newly found purpose and determination, Carry began her campaign by verbally accosting public officials and jointists on the streets of

Medicine Lodge. One of her favorite epithets was, "Hello, you rum-soaked Republican rummy," for she believed the Republican party and especially President William McKinley were in league with the liquor industry. If she met a bar owner on the street, she would greet him with, "How do you do, maker of drunkards and widows."

Soon after Carry's three-day prayer session, a "good Christian woman," Mrs. Eliot, visited her, desperately seeking help. Mrs. Eliot's husband spent each night drinking in a bar owned by Henry Durst. The man had stumbled home drunk the previous night, had kicked over the table, and driven Mrs. Eliot and the three children from the house. Mrs. Eliot had been taking in washing to feed the children, but her husband continually seized the money for his nightly drinking bouts. As a result, there was usually only cornbread and molasses for the family's meals.

The woman's plight must have reminded Carry of the days when David Nation had left the family behind on the Texas ranch with barely any food and also of those lonely nights when she had waited for Charles Gloyd to return from the Masonic Lodge bar. Now, at last, Carry would have a chance to strike back against alcohol.

Immediately, Carry and Mrs. Eliot headed for Durst's joint. Though at the time Carry was uncertain about her course of action, this would be the initial confrontation between her and a bar owner. Her strategy would crystallize further in the months ahead, as she pursued her cause.

When Carry and Mrs. Eliot reached the building, Carry instructed Mrs. Eliot to get on her knees before the front entrance and pray. The sight of two women, kneeling before the door and shrieking prayers, caused a crowd to collect. The five patrons inside the joint scampered out the back door. Infuriated, Durst ordered the women to leave. Carry countered by warning him that she would hold similar prayer meetings twice a day unless he closed down within three days. She augmented this threat by meeting with the local town officials and demanding that they enforce the state law and shut down the illegal business.

Durst closed the bar and subsequently moved to another state. "I heard afterwards," Carry wrote, "that he was reduced to poverty."

Flushed with her initial victory, Carry now eyed the other six drinking establishments as well as the Medicine Lodge drugstores that dispensed alcohol. Along with Mrs. Laurence Cain, the wife of the Baptist minister, Carry worked for a county chapter of the Women's Christian Temperance Union (W.C.T.U.). At the organizational meeting, the group had elected Mrs. Cain president and appointed Carry as jail evangelist. Immediately, she began visiting the local jail, hoping to convert the prisoners.

Though her success as jail evangelist was limited, a new ability became evident through these weekly meetings. The men resisted her religious efforts, but they treated her with kindness and respect. From this point forward, Carry possessed a knack for successfully dealing with persons of all ages and backgrounds. Carry Nation was against many things during her life, and at times her wrath focused on specific individuals, but she basically liked people, and others sensed this quickly.

Personal problems forced Carry to leave Kansas for a month. Her daughter Charlien was pregnant with her fourth child, and her health had never been strong. Carry journeyed to Texas to help Charlien through the last weeks of her pregnancy. Upon arriving, Carry was horrified to discover that both Charlien and her husband, Alexander, had become heavy drinkers. The campaign against alcohol took on new urgency now that the dreaded enemy had again infiltrated Carry's own family.

Returning to Medicine Lodge, Carry continued to harass local officials about the illegal drinking business. Also, she enlisted Mrs. Cain from the Barber County W.C.T.U. and prepared another direct attack. Their target was to be Mart Strong's saloon, the most disreputable and prosperous joint in town.

On a Saturday afternoon late in the summer of 1899, Carry and Mrs. Cain put on their best "black alpaca dresses and most becoming poke bonnets" and headed along the main street. The sight of Mrs. Cain lugging a hand organ and Carry gripping her umbrella with the sharpened point attracted a crowd. Word spread quickly about their mission, and by the time the ladies arrived at Strong's joint, a mob of two hundred persons was waiting to see what would happen. Some had gathered to heckle the two crusaders; others were supporters or members of the W.C.T.U.

"Men and women of Medicine Lodge, this is a joint!" shouted Carry, and she immediately launched into her favorite antiwhiskey song, "Who Hath Sorrow? Who Hath Woe?" The crowd pressed in as the women reached the final chorus, which went:

> "Touch not, taste not, handle not,
> Drink will make the dark, dark blot.
> Like an adder it will sting,
> And at last to ruin bring,
> They who tarry at the drink."

As some of the crowd applauded, Carry led the charge through the front door but was met head on by Mart Strong, who swung her around and pushed her out again. She rushed Strong once more, swinging her umbrella like a sickle. Strong ducked to one side, grabbed Carry, and flung the 175-pound woman out the door so hard that she landed on the sidewalk.

Marshal John Gano, who had been observing the fracas, moved in when he saw Carry sitting on the street, her bonnet tilted over one ear. "Take it easy," he warned Strong.

Carry was on her feet again, urging supporters in the audience to join her battle.

Gano told her, "Now, Mother Nation, don't start trouble. I sure wish I could take you off the streets."

Wheeling about, Carry advanced until only inches separated them. "Yes, you want to take me, a woman whose heart is breaking to see the ruin of these men, the desolate homes and broken laws, and you a constable oath-bound to close this man's unlawful business. Why don't you do your duty?"

Members of the mob shouted agreement, and Gano realized the onlookers were beginning to side with Carry. Gano tried to calm the crowd and suggested that the watchers disperse. Using this distraction, Strong and his patrons locked the front door and erected a barricade of chairs and tables to keep the attackers outside. Some customers became frightened and sneaked out the back door. Carry and Mrs. Cain caught one farmhand as he climbed over the back fence. They hauled him down and flung him to his knees. With Mrs. Cain playing the hand organ, Carry sang, "Yield Not to Temptation" and then lectured the man about the evils of drink.

Strong refused to open his doors again that day, so Carry and Mrs. Cain went home. Some members of the crowd who had been in favor of the encounter visited the mayor and several councilmen that evening, parading and singing outside their homes until the early hours of the morning. Finally, the men agreed that Mart Strong's bar would be closed. Within a few days, Medicine Lodge officials "were surprised" to discover they had several more illegal drinking establishments in town, and they promptly shut them down also.

If the town fathers thought this would still the anti-alcohol voices, however, they were wrong. With the joints out of business, Carry now decided to eliminate the drugstores that sold alcohol openly and with only a pretense of requiring prescriptions. One drugstore in town, operated by Mr. O. L. Day, who did not have an official permit to sell prescription whiskey, seemed the best example. When Carry approached fellow members of the W.C.T.U., however, she found that many of them were hesitant about joining any mission led by Carry Nation. The physical struggle at Strong's bar had gone beyond the pacifist approach advocated by the temperance group. Most members of the Barber County chapter would help only by being vocal supporters outside the store.

Once again Carry would be the leader, and once again Mrs. Cain would act as her lieutenant. The third member of the squad was Mrs. Noble, an amateur horse wrangler. The impetus for the mission came when Carry received a report that a ten-pound keg of liquor had been slipped surreptitiously into Day's back room.

On February 16, 1900, the three women crashed into Day's drugstore and accused him of selling illegal alcohol. The frail man denied this charge. He claimed he was awaiting a permit that would allow him to dispense liquor for medicinal purposes.

Carry called him "a fool and a rummy" and shoved her way past him into the back room. There under the bar, or what Day called his "prescription counter," sat the telltale wooden container.

"Women!" Carry shouted. "*Here* is the whiskey!"

Day argued that the keg contained "fine California brandy," which had cost him seventy-five dollars.

"It's devil's brew to destroy the souls of men!" Carry sat astride the barrel while Day begged the women to leave his store.

Word had reached Marshal Gano that a crowd had collected in front of Day's store to witness Carry's latest foray. At this moment Gano rushed into the building. Day, bolstered by the arrival of help, tried to push Carry off the keg. The six-foot woman one-armed him across the room, where Day crumpled into a corner, dazed. Gano applied a headlock to Carry.

"My neck's breaking!" Carry screamed.

The sound of raucous screams for help impelled Mrs. Cain into action. Gathering a few W.C.T.U. allies, who had now adopted a more militant stance, Mrs. Cain rushed to Carry's defense. Gano, still struggling with the hefty Carry, suddenly felt his jacket being ripped away. Glancing over his shoulder, he saw the angry women were prepared to do more serious harm to his body. Gano decided retreat was the wisest course of action.

The battle was now about over.

"Roll out the broth of hell!" ordered Carry.

The women shoved and kicked the keg into the street. Mrs. Noble ran into a nearby hardware store and demanded a hatchet. The proprietor informed her that he was "in the business of selling hatchets, not giving them away." Denouncing the man as a drunkard, Mrs. Noble crossed the street and entered the blacksmith shop. Selecting the cooperative owner's heaviest mallet, she hurried back to Carry.

Carry gripped the mallet and raised it above her head. The Kansas *Journal* reported that the crowd cheered when she struck the keg "with such force that the liquor streamed out many feet up in the air."

Some shouts came from people who had arrived with cups and other containers, anticipating a free drink. As they moved forward expectantly, Mrs. Cain regrouped her forces.

"Form a line," she yelled to her allies. "Don't anyone touch these women! They are Christian women trying to save the boys of our state."

While the members of the W.C.T.U. blocked the freeloaders' advance, Carry had a woman fill a small bottle with liquor, to be held as proof of Day's crime. Then, quickly, she swept the brandy into the gutter and set the murky brown liquid afire.

Knowing Day's petition for a permit to sell liquor legally would be up for debate within a few weeks, Carry kept the brandy-filled bottle as evidence. If the fact that Day had been selling liquor illegally could be established, he would not receive his license.

During this period Carry's and Mrs. Cain's homes were stoned and all the windows smashed. Also, Carry's buggy was vandalized. Realizing that the hidden forces behind the liquor industry were beginning to get alarmed, Carry became even more determined to push her crusade ahead. A notorious bootlegger was sent to Carry to warn her and the other ladies of the W.C.T.U. that if they brought charges or testified against Day in court, Carry's house would be burned down.

Her answer was, "Should my home be burned, it would be a lecture in favor of my cause that would be worth more than my home."

At the county court hearing on Day's application, Carry appeared, as did her cohorts. She presented the bottle of brandy as evidence of Day's wrongdoing. The proalcohol forces had marshaled the aid of a medical man, Dr. Gould, who testified that Day had purchased the brandy on his recommendation. Despite this, Day's petition was rejected. A few weeks later, he sold the store and moved away.

Solely through Carry Nation's efforts, Medicine Lodge had been transformed into the only dry town in a supposedly dry state. As she prepared to enlarge her campaign throughout Barber County, members of the liquor bloc were taking a second look at her successes. If not exactly alarmed, they were more than a little concerned that one determined woman had managed to close six joints and a number of drugstores in one town.

CHAPTER 8

With Medicine Lodge as dry as the sunbaked banks of the Medicine River, county farms and cowboys now had to travel twenty miles south to Kiowa for their drinking. Kiowa was a wide-open town, which had been a jumping-off point for the Oklahoma land rush of 1889. In 1900, a plethora of saloons operated in the small Kansas town, and many of the inhabitants were unsavory characters with criminal histories. If Carry decided to close down this town, she would face stronger opposition than she had met in Medicine Lodge.

Possibly encouraged by the favorable court decision denying O. L. Day's liquor license, Carry decided to try legal avenues before launching an attack on the notorious Kiowa. First, she visited the Barber County attorney, Samuel Griffen, and stated her belief that Kiowa was a major source of illegal liquor in the county. Griffen would not consider her evidence. Later, Carry attacked the county attorney, via newspapers and public appearances, as being an affiliate of the jointists.

Having failed with Griffen, Carry wrote to A. A. Goddard, the state attorney in Topeka, who had the responsibility to see that all the county attorneys fulfilled the obligations of their positions. He answered Carry with vague letters promising assistance that never materialized.

At last she called upon the governor, William Stanley. "I told him of the prisoners in jail in our county from the sale of liquor in the dives of Kiowa, told him of the broken families and troubles of all kinds . . . told him of the brokenhearted women and the worse than fatherless children."

Governor Stanley refused to help. He was too involved, Carry reported, with a personal campaign against women card players who gambled with "the Devil's pasteboards." Stanley considered these individuals to be "loafers worse than whiskey drinkers or cigarette smokers."

In a state that had a constitutional amendment against saloons, Carry Nation found no government official willing to enforce the written law. She was not naïve; she could pinpoint the reasons. Carry realized a basic fact of political life—that generous supporters of a victorious political party rarely face prosecution. Carry also knew, as many did, that the liquor industry had organized the Mystic Order of Brotherhood, the purpose of which was to work for repeal of the Kansas antisaloon law.

Brewers and distillers all across the United States were diverting large sums of money into the Mystic Order of Brotherhood. "If the liquor men can bring back saloons into Kansas," Carry argued, "then a great blow will have been struck against Prohibition in all the states."

But how was she to prevent this? The initial wave of success in Medicine Lodge, capped by the legal recognition of the court, appeared to promise larger victories. But the promise had not been fulfilled. "I had gone from the lowest to the chief executive of the state, and after appealing to the Governor in vain I found that I could go to no other authority on earth."

Always quick to claim guilt as her own, Carry suffered spells of depression. She wondered if she had in some way failed the heavenly faith invested in her. She engaged in long periods of prayer and fasting and at times dressed in sackcloth and smeared dark ashes on her face.

On the evening of June 5, 1900, Carry prayed in her bedroom, advancing upon her knees as usual. She begged God to "use me to save Kansas . . . please show me something to do." In the morning, she was awakened by a soft chanting voice, which repeated the same phrase over and over: "Go to Kiowa. Go to Kiowa." Her hands were lifted by an unseen power and then released. The voice said, "I'll stand by you."

Carry rose from the bed, dressed, and, taking a burlap sack, went to a nearby field. There she added some rocks to a half dozen bricks she had discovered in her own yard. She wrapped each missile in newspaper and packed them into her buggy. Then she hitched up her horse, Prince, and confidently set off for Kiowa and, unknown to her at the time, the national temperance scene.

The temperance debate in the United States had raged since 1808, when twenty-three citizens of Saratoga County, New York, formed the first American temperance society to oppose hard liquor. Twenty-six years later the first national temperance convention met in Philadelphia. Maine was the first state to go dry in 1846, followed between 1851 and 1855 by what are called the "First Wave" states: Connecticut, Delaware, Indiana, Iowa, Massachusetts, Michigan, Minnesota, Nebraska, New Hampshire, New York, Rhode Island, and Vermont. However, like certain individuals who renounce drink and then succumb again to the temptation, all these states were later to repeal their laws.

Meanwhile, an impression had been made on the nation's conscience, and the National Prohibition party was organized in 1869. The effect was that the "Second Wave" of state prohibition occurred in the years just before Carry's efforts in Medicine Lodge and Kiowa. Five states joined Kansas with laws forbidding the sale of alcohol.

As Carry Nation, dressed in her Sunday best, guided Prince through Medicine Lodge and onto a dirt road, she was totally unknown outside her county. She was a single individual waging a fight while, throughout the country, large organizations and a political party were struggling to bring about their goals with only minimal success. Nevertheless, Prince trotted on, bearing his mistress toward a destiny in which she would overshadow all previous efforts and become the single most dominant antialcohol force in the world.

The small buggy bounced along the road, which twisted and curved among white boulders, cottonwoods, and patches of golden sunflowers. About a mile south of town, Carry squinted through the yellow dust and twirling tumbleweeds. Before her she saw a mob of devils, men with horns and cloven hooves, who were blocking the bridge. They were jumping about and brandishing sharp-pronged spears.

"O God, help me!" implored Carry.

CARRY NATION

Prince trotted straight for the devils as Carry repeated her plea. Suddenly the clouds parted, and a dazzling beam of light shone through. A large figure with a brilliantly glowing halo appeared in the light, mounted on a white horse. The figure gestured menacingly at the dancing devils on the bridge, and they vanished into swirls of dust.

Carry accepted the vision as proof of what the voice had told her earlier that day. *I'll stand by you.* As she journeyed toward Kiowa, her spirits were uplifted and she felt like Joan of Arc. In future years she would often publicly note the similarity between herself and the French maiden as further proof of the goodness of her own holy mission.

That night Carry stayed with a fellow W.C.T.U. member, Mrs. Springer, who lived five miles south of Kiowa. She was careful not to explain her purpose because the conservative temperance organization would not have approved of her methods.

On Monday morning, Carry arrived in Kiowa at eight o'clock, her buggy filled with rocks, or what she called "smashers." Spotting Dobson's Saloon, she tucked a number of the missiles into the crook of her arm and marched into the bar, which already had a few customers.

"Men!" she exclaimed. "I have come to save you from a drunkard's fate!"

Whether or not Carry achieved this purpose is unknown, but a half hour later Dobson's Saloon was in shambles. The huge gilt-edge mirror had been shattered, as had all the glasses and bottles in sight. Even an armchair rocker had been splintered by the last of Carry's bricks.

Mission accomplished, Carry turned to Dobson,

who crouched in a corner, eyes wide with fright. "I have finished. God be with you."

Carry was not finished, however, for when she reached the curb, she picked up several large stones and shattered the plate-glass window of the saloon. On she went to the next joint. Her attack here was so swift and unexpected that the owner later said he thought the devil himself had visited his place until he heard Carry's last words, "God be with you." The proprietor was in such a state of anger or shock that he snatched up one of Carry's "smashers" and destroyed a window that she had overlooked.

The next stop was the Lewis Bar, where a teenage boy was working as bartender.

"Young man, come from behind that bar!" Carry shouted. "Your mother did not raise you for such a place."

When the youth hesitated, Carry motivated him into action by hurling a billiard ball with such controlled aim that the ball missed his head by inches. The young man crouched and duck-waddled for safety. Methodically and with deadly precision, Carry let loose a barrage of rocks, breaking everything made of glass, including a long bar mirror. Then she flipped over tables and chairs, ripped sporting prints from the walls, and shattered windows.

Carry emerged from the building to find that "by this time the streets were crowded with people. Most of them seemed to look puzzled." The audience might well have been mystified to see this six-foot woman, her bonnet tilting, her hands filthy, her black alpaca dress soaked with alcohol. Carry stood there a moment, breathing deeply and sweating, while the Kansas sun beat down on her whiskey-and-beer-stained dress. The odor of liquor was overpowering even from many feet away.

"Men of Kiowa, I have destroyed three of your places of business! If I have broken a statute of Kansas, put me in jail. If I am not a lawbreaker, your Mayor and Councilmen are. You must arrest one of us."

With an accuracy to match her rock-throwing talent, Carry had neatly placed the local officials in an awkward situation. Can someone be arrested for destroying property that is illegal? If such a person is placed on trial, then the court would be forced to judge the legality of the saloons. This would mean the eventual shutdown of Kiowa's joints.

In what must have been a comic show for the several hundred onlookers, Carry, Mayor Korn, and the angry saloon owners stayed in one group, while a hundred feet away the town attorney and the councilmen hovered in conference. Runners raced back and forth between the clusters, bearing messages that sought to arrive at an equitable solution. But Carry had the bargaining advantage, and she knew it. Not only did the public officials want to avoid the knotty legal problem, they also preferred that news of the day's episodes not reach the Kansas or out-of-state papers. Unfortunately, they did not realize they were dealing with a person who would soon be a master at gaining publicity.

With what can only be viewed as typical political oversight, the mayor and councilmen decided nothing had happened in town that day. The marshal ordered Carry to return to Medicine Lodge and never again appear in Kiowa. If she ever came back, he would put her in jail.

Not intimidated by this threat, Carry replied, "Unless you close all the dives, I'll be back."

CARRY NATION

Despite the efforts of the Kiowa officials, accounts of Carry's saloon smashing appeared in all the large Kansas papers as well as in a few from nearby states. Carry was deluged with offers to speak or smash joints in the hometowns of the letter writers. Some invitations were ludicrous. She was offered five hundred dollars to wrestle a grizzly bear in Montana, and a saloon wanted her as a bouncer for a guaranteed salary plus all the free liquor she could drink. Carry did accept the invitations to speak, though she turned the other proposals down, including one from a theatrical stock company that wanted her to appear in *Ten Nights in a Barroom*.

Her Kiowa attack had even more pronounced results. A wave of prohibition swept the county. Fellow members of the Barber County W.C.T.U., and many individuals who had always been opposed to alcohol but had never spoken out against it, now began to make public demands. Carry and her newfound allies brought the cases of the Kiowa jointists to court, and all the bar owners were found guilty and ordered to shut down. Nearby communities, frightened by this public upsurge, suddenly discovered illegal joints within their borders and closed them down quickly. Barber County became the only dry county in a theoretically dry state, and this happened solely through Carry Nation's efforts.

The success was not without its price. County Attorney Griffen brought suit against Carry for malicious slander, citing her public statements that he was involved with the jointists. Though Carry had letters and testimony to prove that Griffen had gambled and had been seen drinking in dives, the court found her guilty. Though she was only fined one dollar, the court-assigned legal costs amounted to two hundred dollars. Carry did not have the money, so a lien was placed against her house. Several years would pass before she could raise enough cash to do away with the lien.

Another blow came when the state and national organizations of the W.C.T.U. disclaimed any connection with Carry Nation because she did not adhere to that group's philosophy. Most of Carry's friends from her own chapter, however, did not desert her.

All this opposition served only to fire Carry's drive. She selected Wichita, the home base of the Republican party bosses and the jointists, as her next target.

Obsessed with the belief that she would not survive this particular battle, Carry made what she considered her final appearances at the three churches in Medicine Lodge. Then, in preparation for Wichita, she discarded her previous weapons of rocks and decided to employ an iron rod twelve inches long "and as large around as my thumb." As an auxiliary weapon, she selected one of David's heaviest canes. After the near arrest in Kiowa, Carry anticipated she might not elude the law this time, so she packed a valise with some personal articles and the family Bible.

Though she had not yet settled upon the weapon that would become the symbol of Carry Nation, her battle uniform was now set and would remain the same for the rest of her life. The next morning Carry rose at sunrise and put on her black alpaca dress with the large black pearl buttons up one side and a dark poke bonnet, secured with a silk ribbon under her chin. In cooler weather, such as Kansas was now experiencing, she also wore a dark-blue serge cloak.

Thus clad and fully armed, Carry Nation boarded the Santa Fe train for Wichita and her first imprisonment.

CHAPTER 9

The train pulled into Wichita at seven o'clock that evening. As soon as Carry had registered at a hotel near the depot, she went out to reconnoiter the situation. Walking down the street, she passed many suspicious-looking businesses with heavily curtained windows and signs that announced they were "sample rooms."

"I went into about fourteen places where men were drinking at bars . . . the police standing with the others." Outraged by the obvious illegality, Carry continued her tour and found the Hotel Carey. The Annex Bar in the hotel was one of the finest drinking establishments in the country, second only to the Alcazar Saloon in Peoria, Illinois, with its floor and bar rail made of marble and black onyx. The splendor may have been the motivation for Carry's selecting the Hotel Carey Annex as her target. Also, she did have a knack for getting publicity, and she may well have realized that newspaper reporters could have fun with the similarity in the names of the attacker and the attacked.

Later, she claimed her decision was caused by an incident that occurred as she stood in the doorway, surveying the future battlefield. An unshaven, shabbily dressed man entered the Annex and requested a drink.

The bartender glanced disdainfully at him. "Get out. You disgrace my place."

The tramp "who had been his mother's greatest treasure" started toward the door. At that moment, a well-dressed young man entered. The bartender promptly prepared a drink and handed the glass to the new customer.

The ne'er-do-well stopped in the doorway and called to the bartender, "Five years ago I came into your place looking just like that young man. You have made me what you see now. Give that drink to me and finish your work."

According to Carry, that was the exact moment when she decided that the Annex would be the first bar in Wichita she would visit the next day. Angry, she returned to her hotel, where she bound together the iron rod and the cane in order to make a stronger club. For several hours that night she prayed, advancing upon her knees.

The next morning, December 27, 1900, with her cane-rod and "some of the nicest rocks, round with sharp edges" hidden beneath her cloak, Carry sallied forth to confront the enemy. Discussion has raged about how Carry was able to hide so much beneath her cape. One biographer has theorized that Carry, an expert seamstress, had sewn pockets into the lining.

She arrived at the hotel, where Edward Park was tending bar in the Annex and serving seven early-morning customers. Carry entered and glanced around the elegantly decorated room. The walls and ceiling were gray stucco blocks which had come from the buildings of the 1893 Chicago World's Fair. The fifty-foot curved bar was constructed from highly polished cherry wood. A long Victorian mirror graced the wall behind the bar and there were beautiful cut-glass decanters filled with liquor. Shining cherry-wood tables alternated with tall brass spittoons throughout the seating area. However, the decoration that seized Carry's attention was a life-size painting of a naked woman, "Cleopatra at the Bath." This picture of the Egyptian queen surrounded by seminude Roman and Egyptian maidens seemed to symbolize for Carry the evilness of the Annex.

Removing a rock from underneath her cloak, Carry aimed carefully. The stone smashed the glass covering the painting and punctured the canvas. Carry immediately hurled another rock, but it was to be one of the few times a Carry Nation missile went wild. The poor throw bothered her for years. "I wish I had thought and thrown another at the face of the picture so it could not have been repaired," she later wrote.

With the outbreak of violence, bartender Parker dropped a bottle of whiskey, which smashed on the floor. "Stop it!" he ordered.

Carry stood in the doorway, "a six-foot, 180-pound female with broad shoulders and hips. Her thin lips were pursed under a flat, round nose, her black, piercing eyes glared furiously. . . ." Wheeling, she threw another rock, which shattered the fifteen-hundred-dollar mirror.

The battle was on!

Shouting, "Peace on earth! Goodwill to men," Carry ran up and down the length of the bar, swinging her club. Glasses, bottles, and the chandelier were smashed, and huge dents were hacked into the cherry-wood bar. The customers dived behind the bar, where Parker was already hiding. At one point, he got up and begged Carry to stop, but he quickly ducked again when a beer bottle crashed onto the shelf above his head.

When Detective Park Massey arrived, he found Carry repeatedly beating a brass spitton on the bar. Taking her arm, he announced he was placing her under arrest. She yanked herself free and tried to hit Massey over the head with the club.

"Arrest me?" she yelled. "Why don't you arrest the man who runs this hellhole? Don't you know this is against the law? Can't you smell the rotten poison?"

Massey confiscated the club and escorted Carry from the building. All the way to police headquarters, Carry sang, "Am I a Soldier of the Cross?"

The chief of police told Carry that he was surprised to learn that a joint was selling liquor in Wichita. He would certainly attend to that matter. However, if Carry would take the next train back to Medicine Lodge and never return to Wichita, he would release her.

Carry laughed and vowed to smash every saloon in the city.

For the rest of the day, she remained in a locked room at police headquarters while the city officials decided how to handle the situation. As in Kiowa, the men knew that bringing the case to court would result in bad publicity and unpleasant legal ramifications.

At six thirty that evening the county attorney, Samuel Amidon, decided to prosecute Carry. The charge was "malicious destruction of property" in "a certain part of the Hotel Carey." Amidon hoped that this ambiguous wording would prevent Carry from bringing up the fact that the Annex was an illegal business, but when she appeared in court, Carry asked that the charge be changed from malicious destruction of property to "destruction of malicious property." She also insisted upon calling Judge O. D. Kirk "Your Dishonor."

The exasperated judge set the trial for January 5, 1901, and remanded Carry to Sedgwick County Jail. Carry was escorted there and locked in "the Rotary," which was the section reserved for the most dangerous criminals. The Rotary was a revolving cage of twelve wedge-shaped compartments. Each cell was so small that only a cot, a chair, and a tiny table could fit into the filthy cubicle.

"The sensation of being locked in such a place for the first time is not like any other," Carry later wrote. She grasped the steel bars and shook them, crying and moaning. "You have put me in here a cub, but I will come out roaring like a lion, and I will make all hell howl."

The commotion inside the country jail was mild compared to the effect on Wichita. People gathered on street corners, discussing the wrecked bar and questioning everyone they met about the rumored trainloads of Carry's friends already on the way to smash more joints. Others predicted that Carry's attack was only the first skirmish in a liquor war between prohibitionists and saloonkeepers.

In some ways the rumors were accurate. Many of Carry's friends were traveling to Wichita, but not to lead more attacks. They wished to help her legally and to give her moral support during the trial. The first arrivals remained in the jail corridors during the night, singing hymns and praying loudly.

If Carry's assault on the Annex wasn't the beginning of a liquor war, the attack was her first major offensive in a national war against alcohol. Her Kiowa adventures had spread her name throughout Kansas and a few neighboring states. Wichita brought Carry nationwide fame. Reporters descended upon the city and the jail, sending her statements about jointists, hell's broth, and Republican rummies to their newspapers all over the country. Letters and telegrams flowed into the jail. Women applauded her campaign. Ministers held prayer meetings for her and sent donations to offset her legal fees.

As with any well-known person, not all the letters were positive. Carry later reported, "I never knew until then that people thought or could write such vile things . . . the most horrible infidelity, cursing God, threatening me."

The personnel of the Sedgwick County Jail had never witnessed such goings-on: reporters clamoring for interviews, ladies singing and praying, sacks of mail and telegrams. An even stranger transformation was to take place in the weeks that Carry was held prisoner. When she was first locked into the Rotary with the drunks, murderers, and rustlers, the sheriff encouraged the other prisoners to light up cigarettes and pipes. He instructed them to puff the smoke into Carry's cell. Despite Carry's protests, the men continued to torment her.

Late one night shortly after her incarceration, Carry heard several prisoners swearing. She shook the cell bars and shouted at them. "What do you boys mean by asking God to damn this place? I think He has already done so, and I don't want any more 'damns' here. Get down on your knees and ask God to bless you."

For the rest of the night, the cell block was quiet.

While in jail, Carry would again display her ability to meet people on their own level and to find goodness in everyone. At times the men joked about her hymn singing and praying. Carry took the gibes good-naturedly, joining in the humor and camaraderie, although she couldn't resist answering them with lectures on religion. Even though the men were constantly kidding her, Carry spent the last of her own money to buy fruit and butter for the needy prisoners because the jail meals were so poor.

Several days later she was pleased to hear several prisoners singing a hymn. "How are you, boys?" she called out.

"We've all been converted."

Carry realized that total conversion was a bit improbable, but she recognized the answer as an attempt by her fellow prisoners to make her feel better. Soon after came the three-day period when a sheet of paper was mysteriously slipped from cell to cell, and the men argued over words such as whiskey, sin, and angel. At last the paper was handed to Carry. The inmates had composed a poem, "Solemn Thoughts," as a tribute to her. The nine stanzas described her as a "Christian martyr" and the other prisoners as "deep-strained in sin." Carry was reported as "singing songs of Christ's dear love" and praying. The fourth stanza read:

> "Some who'd never known a mother,
>   Ne'er had learned to kneel and pray,
> Raised their hands, their face to cover,
>   Till her words had died away."

A prisoner who was released while Carry was in jail came to bid her good-bye. He explained that the prisoners' statement that they had been converted was true. He attributed this to their respect for the brave way she was acting.

Other individuals were not impressed with Carry's

performance—the liquor men. Carry's attack and much-publicized jailing had taken place only a few days before the state legislature was to begin considering the question of repealing the antisaloon law. The proalcohol politicians decided to isolate Carry from her supporters and especially from the newsmen until a vote had been taken on abolishing prohibition. So they prepared a statement, which was released to the newspapers, declaring that Isaiah Cooper, a man in the cell next to Carry, had been exposed to smallpox. The jail was placed under strict quarantine for the next three weeks, and Carry's trial was postponed.

To the dismay of the saloonists, the scheme backfired and created the very result they wished to avoid. Carry now had attained the status of a true martyr, and public indignation spread. The phony quarantine also raised the ire of the national organization of the W.C.T.U., which up to this point had quietly ignored Carry. The group hired a physician, who went to the jail and examined Cooper. The doctor stated that the man was in good health and could not possibly have been exposed to smallpox. When the W.C.T.U. brought this fact to the attention of Judge Kirk, he still refused to lift the quarantine.

Mrs. Lillian Stevens, the national president of the W.C.T.U., released a statement that received wide press coverage. "Kansas is a prohibition state, and the laws should be enforced. If no other means were possible, I believe Mrs. Nation's course was justifiable."

Following this declaration of backing came an announcement from Miss Eva Marshall, president of the American Young People's Christian Temperance Union. "What could that woman do, if she wanted her home protected, but take the law in her own hands?"

To compound the burgeoning support for Carry,

CARRY NATION

David Nation arrived in Wichita and joined the W.C.T.U's legal staff in presenting her plea for habeas corpus to the Kansas Supreme Court. "The Carrie [sic] Nation case has reached the capital," reported the Topeka *Journal.*

The Wichita politicians were frantic. Everything was going wrong for them, and every day the Carry Nation case was becoming more of a problem for national concern. Obviously, Carry had to be dealt with in another way, and quickly.

Now Carry's friendship with the prisoners began to reap benefits. Carry had befriended the trusty of the jail, John, by giving him her last four dollars because she had learned that his wife had no money for food.

One day John brought news about Dodd, the jailkeeper. "Something is in the wind," the trusty said. "All sorts of important people are seeing Dodd."

Soon after, Dodd came to Carry's cell and explained that she was to be released. "A cab will be waiting at the back of the jail. Your trials are over."

However, John warned her, "Don't leave the jail. There is some plot going on and they mean mischief."

That night Carry obtained several loops of strong wire from John and tied the cell door to the nearby bars and then to the legs of the cot. She snapped off one cot leg and gripped it like a club. Carry sat up all night, "waiting for someone to come in my cell to drag me out. With the cot leg I was going to strike their hands if they attempted to open the door."

The night passed without any incident.

No one is certain as to exactly what the plotters had in mind for Carry. One theory was that they simply meant to sneak her out of Wichita and deposit her back in Medicine Lodge. Another possibility was that they would bring her to a mental hospital and have her declared insane. Whatever the goal, the scheme failed. The ill-fated plot was the last opportunity for the proalcohol forces of Wichita.

On January 12, the Kansas Supreme Court ruled that Carry should be released on $200 bail. Six days later all charges were dismissed and Carry was freed. David brought her to the nearby village of Newton so that she could rest from her experiences.

The period of recuperation was brief. Within the week Carry was invited by Wichita's W.C.T.U. chapter to appear at a meeting. During the session, Carry delivered a speech that fired the group so thoroughly that everyone decided to go forth and wreck more joints. Carry and a few others stopped at the home of Mrs. Julie Evans for last-minute preparations. While there, Carry went to the basement and returned with a weapon that was to become her hallmark.

On January 21, 1901, almost nineteen years to the day before Prohibition would become a national law, Carry Nation walked into the streets of Wichita—hatchet in hand.

CHAPTER 10

Carry had selected three assistants to accompany her: Mrs. Lucy Wilhoite, Mrs. Lydia Muntz, and Mrs. Julia Evans. The quartet swooped down upon a saloon belonging to James Burns. Within minutes they had demolished the interior and were on their way to John Herrig's Palace Café. In the midst of this second attack, however, Herrig waved a revolver and threatened to shoot Carry if she and her cohorts did not leave. The women retreated to the street. There, a crowd of about three thousand people milled about. Every Wichita policeman available had been placed on emergency duty to prevent a large-scale riot. Carry led her friends to the Carey Hotel, but the doors were locked and special guards hired by the owners prevented a forced entry.

With the mob becoming more unruly, the police brought the four crusaders to headquarters. The chief of police said he would release them if they promised not to do any more smashing until noon the next day. Honor-bound to abstain from further wrecking in Wichita, Carry decided to leave for Enterprise, Kansas. While in jail she had received numerous letters from women in

Enterprise describing how their husbands were addicted to drink and frequented the Enterprise joints. Also, the name of the small town appealed to her much as the Carey Hotel had a week before. Carry packed a few rocks, the iron rod, and her newly found weapon—the hatchet—and set off for the railroad station that evening. She planned to stay only a short time in Enterprise and then to move on quickly to Topeka, where she could fight the possible repeal of the antisaloon law.

Meanwhile, the county authorities had issued a warrant for her arrest. As Carry was purchasing her train ticket, Sheriff Simmons took her arm. "Madam, you are under arrest."

Swinging around, Carry screamed, "Ahab!" and smacked him in the face. Then she grabbed Simmons by his ears and shook the short man while the women in the crowded depot danced about and shrieked. By the time the police came to the sheriff's assistance, Carry was "literally dragging him about the waiting-room by the ears."

For the next few days Carry and two of her W.C.T.U. allies were held in the county jail, while the city officials seriously considered placing Wichita under martial law. Gangs of drunken men wandered through the streets, angrily discussing the raids upon their masculine strongholds, the joints. In counterpoint, the women were singing and holding impromptu prayer meetings on street corners. Minor incidents of smashing and looting by persons of both persuasions were reported. One night a mob of one hundred men gathered before the jail, yelling, "Lynch Carry Nation!" The police were called to break up the crowd, the extra jail guards remained on duty at all times.

Five days later prohibition workers posted bail for

the three women. Word had spread that Carry was to be freed, and a noisy crowd had collected. The police waited until dark to release Carry, but even then the whole town seemed to be waiting for her. As she stepped from the door, hoots and obscenities were showered upon her.

The police formed a wedge and tried to move her safely to the railroad station. The mob was angry and becoming more dangerous. A large group of Salvation Army members assisted the police by forming a hollow box around Carry as she walked toward the depot. Once she was safely aboard the train, Carry opened the window to wave and give a final message. Rotten eggs flew through the air, but the window slid down and Carry was not splattered. Someone hurled a rock, which smashed the glass, but again, Carry escaped injury. She sat there, smiling and praying as all the other occupants of the railroad car fled to another coach.

The train lurched forward, and Carry was on her way, leaving behind a city gone mad.

Her effect on Enterprise was equally powerful. Along with several W.C.T.U. women, Carry chopped a swath through one joint, gave a street-corner speech, which erupted into an egg-throwing riot, and then led an attack on the next saloon. The jointists' wives and the prostitutes who worked in the dives were there and attacked Carry with whips and clubs. When no one else came to Carry's aid, the mother of one of the jointists drove back the band of women. Someone helped Carry to her feet. Her black dress was splotched with rotten eggs, her bonnet lay in the dirt, and blood streamed down her face.

Carry glanced at the W.C.T.U. ladies now battling the prostitutes, at the gangs of drunken men arguing, and at the smashed windows everywhere. "There is a spirit of anarchy abroad in this town," she observed.

The sentence was an understatement, for not only was Enterprise in chaos, but the whole state of Kansas was slowly approaching the brink of civil war. In the city Carry had just left, two hundred women had held a mass meeting in the Salvation Army barracks and issued a warning that unless all of Wichita's barrooms were shut down, the streets would "run red with blood." At the same time, county leaders in Abilene, hearing that Carry might visit that town, were hastily closing all the joints in the county. In other sections of the state, too, the antiliquor law was for the first time beginning to be enforced.

Leaving the citizens of Enterprise to pick up the pieces, Carry set out for Topeka. She arrived by train on the afternoon of January 26, 1901. Though met by friends, she allowed herself to be ushered to the main waiting room, where reporters and two hundred other people waited to see the woman who had become, almost overnight, one of the most-talked-about individuals in the United States. Her second raid upon Wichita had garnered a full column on the front page of *The New York Times* under the headline "Mrs. Nation Begins Her Crusade Anew."

The newspaper gave her another front-page headline after her visit to Enterprise, announcing, "Mrs. Nation Horsewhipped."

That evening she toured a sampling of Topeka's one hundred joints. Some bars were tightly locked up, but in others, the owners joked with her when she warned them they would soon feel the effects of "hatchetation," a term she had lately coined to describe her attacks. The next few days were spent in a flurry of public speeches, in an invasion of the governor's office, and in the collection of a few stalwart allies who were willing to accompany her on a hatchet-swinging mission. In preparation, six brand-new hatchets were purchased at the Topeka Cash Store for $2.50 apiece.

Carry still bore battle scars from Enterprise. One eye was purple and her face was scratched, but her energy seemed limitless. Though fifty-four years old, Carry had remarkable recuperative powers. David Nation had recently arrived in Topeka and told reporters that when Carry smashed the saloons of Kiowa, "she came home covered with blood, and I thought she had been shot, but she had only cut her hands on broken bottles. I wanted to send for the doctor, but she said the Lord would heal her wounds, and sure enough in a day's time there was not one scar left."

But new scars awaited Carry. A heavy Kansas snowstorm did little to discourage her, but she did encounter one minor problem. Although Topeka abounded with saloons, most joints were of the plank-bar variety with plain chairs and tables as the only furnishings. An attack on a joint of this sort would have little lasting effect, because another old board could be set up and the bar would be open for business again.

Through a process of elimination, Carry discovered the one bar in the city worthy of her attention. The Senate Bar was Topeka's finest and was located at 406 Kansas Avenue, literally in the shadow of the state capitol. The clientele included many of the state's most important legislators.

Early on the morning of February 5, Carry and two lieutenants, Mrs. John White and Miss Madeline Southard, set off through a blinding snowfall for the Senate Bar. The bartender, Benner Tucker, was cheerfully polishing glasses for the anticipated chilled customers who would demand hot toddies. Tucker later claimed the first indication he had that the bar was under attack came when he heard the jangle of broken glass and a thump as a hatchet bit into the bar. Glancing up, Tucker saw that Miss Southard had wrecked the cigar case while Carry and Mrs. White were chopping away at the bar.

Tucker snatched a gun from under the bar and moved toward the women. As he advanced, Carry swung her hatchet, but Tucker dodged the swinging weapon and then grabbed the hatchet from her hand. Firing two shots into the ceiling, Tucker raced out the back door.

Obtaining another weapon from Mrs. White, Carry went about her latest "hatchetation" episode in deadly earnestness. With each swing of the gleaming hatchet, she shouted, "For your sake, Jesus."

One blow destroyed the five-hundred-dollar bar mirror. The long row of liquor bottles and decanters were dragged from the sideboard and systematically smashed. Carry hefted the heavy iron cash register above her head and hurled it into the snowy street. This one feat impressed the gathering crowd outside more than any other. A reporter later wrote that "no average man in good condition could have plucked the machine from its stand."

Carry then slashed the rubber tube that carried the beer from the tanks to the bar faucets. Holding the severed tube like a garden hose, she sprayed beer over the floor and walls and, inadvertently, over herself and her cohorts. The three women dug the bungs from six beer kegs, letting more sudsy foam stream in all directions. The Senate Bar was a tangle of wreckage and its attackers were ankle deep in beer.

A policeman, Officer Graham, "sauntered in" and said, "Well, Sister Nation, I guess I'll have to arrest you." Later Carry would write that "it was one of the nicest arrests I ever had."

Carry turned to her squad. "Everything cleaned up, ladies?"

"Sister Nation, there's nothing left to *smash!*" wailed Miss Southard.

"All right," Carry told the officer. "You came just when I wanted you to." She led the procession into the thickly falling snow, shouting, "Glory to God! Peace on earth, goodwill to men."

At police headquarters, Carry's two companions were released and she was brought before Judge Magraw. The judge listed the charge as disturbing the peace.

"I was not violent but peaceable," Carry argued.

Switching tactics, the judge tried to read the complete law from a legal volume, but Carry called out, "You might as well read a novel to me as that stuff. It doesn't cover my case."

"Do you plead guilty?" the exasperated man asked.

"If you're trying to ask me if I smashed the joint, I rather think I did smash it."

This was not a recognizable plea in Magraw's opinion, so he adjourned the hearing until February 7. Carry was released on a one-hundred-dollar bond with the suggestion she seek legal counsel.

Leaving police headquarters, Carry conducted a series of sidewalk speeches for reporters and the citizens of Topeka. At one point she stopped and read a proclamation to the schoolchildren of America, which she had composed while waiting to appear before Judge Magraw:

CARRY NATION

My precious Little Children:

I send you greetings and ask you to help me destroy that which is on the streets and protected by the police and the city officials to destroy you, my darlings. I want everyone of you little ones to grab a rock and smash up the glass doors and windows of these hell-holes. You will do your duty and enroll your names on the pages of undying fame and place yourself on the side of God and humanity.

Her last speech was made from the steps of the Topeka post office. As she was finishing with a threat to return and demolish all the city's joints, a man rushed from the crowd and presented her with a handful of miniature pewter hatchets.

"You sell these to the crowd, Carry, and you can pay all your fines and costs this month."

Holding up the small gray hatchets, Carry sold them all for ten cents each within minutes. The man's gift was an inspiration, and within a few days Carry had made arrangements with a Providence, Rhode Island, manufacturer for mass production of the souvenirs.

"The little hatchets," she later wrote, "have been my faithful little defenders. They had paid my railroad fares, hotel bills, and they aided me in paying for a home for drunkards' wives." The going rate for a Carry Nation souvenir was twenty-five to fifty cents, depending upon the financial status of the buyer.

On February 7, friends accompanied Carry to police court, where they heard all the city charges against her dropped. The county and state authorities were more persistent, and Carry was ordered to appear in district court on February 18. The dismissal of the city charges, however, was considered a major victory. Carry led her followers from the courtroom, singing, "Praise God From Whom All Blessings Flow." The judge rapped his gavel and the bailiffs shouted for order. The chief of police took no action, so the hymn continued until the final words, when Carry yelled out, "Good-bye," Your Dishonor," and vanished through the doors.

Proceeding directly to the state legislature, Carry demanded to be allowed to speak to both the senate and the representatives.

Nervously, they granted her permission. No one was certain whether Carry had come to speak or to demonstrate hatchetation so, as she stood on the side of the room, waiting her turn to speak, a wave of uneasiness swept through the men.

The apprehension especially affected a clerk reading a bill. The Topeka *State Journal* reported, "At the desk the reading clerk lost his measured tone and broke down repeatedly." The bill the man was reading was a proposed law about fish. "It took him three valiant attempts to say fish hatcheries." First came "fitch hasheries" and then "hash fisheries" and finally, with the legislators laughing over "hass fitcheries," the clerk fled from the room. If nothing else, the poor man's embarrassing experience relaxed many of the lawmakers so that they were more receptive to Carry when she stepped before them and began speaking.

"I've been forced to do this smashing business—I'm going to tell the truth to you—because you haven't been doing your duty. . . . I'm telling you boys to smash the saloons because they are the father of the man who should be educated right. I tell you to smash the saloons or the saloons will smash you."

Carry was loudly cheered at the conclusion of her address. The men present had heard more than Carry Nation speaking to them. They had heard the groundswell of public opinion caused by Carry's "hatchetation." Prohibitionism was sweeping the state with renewed militarism, and if these lawmakers did not want to get swept from office by its vigor, they knew they had better heed this dynamic woman's message. A representative even introduced a bill to legalize saloon smashing, and, though it did not pass, the bill was given a solid positive vote. Even though the resolution never entered the law books, its near passage achieved Carry's goal. The possibility of repealing the constitutional amendment against saloons was now doomed.

Immensely pleased with her success as a speaker, Carry decided to try a new route. Mr. A. C. Rankin, a professional temperance lecturer, offered her seven hundred dollars a week to embark on a speaking tour to Des Moines, Omaha, and eventually Chicago. So, almost one year from the day that she and her friends had destroyed the keg of brandy at O. L. Day's drugstore, Carry packed her bags and set off to strike out against alcohol from the boards of a lecture platform.

CHAPTER 11

Two events occurred in Topeka on February 7, 1901—
the night before Carry embarked on the tour—
that would have a future effect on her life. Seventy
businessmen met and voted unanimously to close down
every saloon, using force, if necessary. A meeting was
set for three days later. At this second meeting, three
thousand people jammed the auditorium and approved
a warning to jointists that they must shut down within
forty-eight hours and ship all bar fixtures and liquor out
of Topeka by February 15. The selection of this date was
propitious though unpremeditated, for no one realized
that Carry would return to the city on February 14.

Also, on the evening of the seventh, David Nation
came to Carry wearing a new blue serge suit, which he
had purchased especially for the tour.

Carry, however, would not let him accompany her.
"No, Papa. You're too old for this trip. You go back to
Medicine Lodge and take care of the place while I'm
away."

This denial was the latest in a long list of denials,
and David returned to Medicine Lodge insulted and
angry. When he had hurried to Wichita and Topeka,

110

Carry had ignored his advice and, even worse, had excluded him from her lectures, where he had hoped to be a speaker. The only job she would entrust to David was sorting her mail and replying to those letters that did not merit her personal attention.

Two days after Carry had embarked upon her lecture series, David told newspaper reporters that she had become domineering and had humiliated him beyond further endurance. The New York *Journal* openly conjectured about a possible divorce. Though the newspaper was premature, the warning signs were there.

Carry, however, already had one successful lecture behind her and was on her way to the next public appearance, so she was probably unaware of David's remarks. At the Academy of Music in Kansas City, she had been introduced as "the finest and noblest woman in Kansas" and had received three rousing cheers from the audience. She informed them that even though Missouri had no antisaloon law, the joints menaced the peace, prosperity, and the pursuit of happiness guaranteed by the Constitution. Her call for the formation of a law-and-order league to enforce Missouri's regulations, such as Sunday and late-hour closings, was acted upon immediately. The new organization chose a hatchet pin as its emblem.

Then Carry was off on a whistle-stop tour of southwestern Iowa, where sympathetic crowds greeted her with flowers and applause. Women held up babies for the crusader to kiss, and men jostled each other, straining to shake hands with her.

In Adair, Iowa, she cried out, "Yes, I'm really Carry Nation. You don't need to doubt it. I'm the saloon smasher. I don't look like it, do I? But I did it with my little hatchet."

In Casey, Iowa: "My dear Sisters and Brothers, I

hope that each of you will take a rock and throw it through the window of any saloon you may find in this town. This crusade has only started."

And so it went, in Anita, Earlham, and other small towns. On February 9, the train pulled into Des Moines, where, *The New York Times* reported, five thousand cheering people met her and a brass band thumped away. Several days later, Carry learned the musicians had been sent by the Bartenders Association as a good-natured joke.

A reporter asked her about a statement by Mayor Harrison of Chicago, in which the mayor had said that she would be severely punished if she did any smashing while in the Windy City.

"Mr. Carter Harrison would better mind his own business," replied Carry. "I think he's the biggest devil in the land."

The police needed a half hour to clear the way for Carry's carriage to proceed to the Kirkwood Hotel. All along the route throngs pressed forward to catch a glimpse of the famous lady.

Not all the residents of Des Moines were thrilled by Carry's visit, however. Many frightened saloon owners hired guards, barricaded their doors, or shut down for the day. One ingenious man, Mr. Romani, rigged a booby trap inside the front entrance of his bar. He filled a large wire cage with fifty half-starved rats and mice and had a connecting string to pull if Carry walked through the doorway, but his inventive thinking was wasted because Carry never inspected his saloon. Meanwhile, many of the caged mice and rats had attacked and killed each other.

The lecture tour ended in Chicago. At the W.C.T.U. Willard Hall, an audience of fifteen hundred enthusiastic supporters waited for Carry, and hundreds more clustered around the outside of the building. The overcrowded conditions and the emotionalism created a health hazard. The women fighting their way in to see the famous reformer shrieked and wept, some fainted. Rescuers had a difficult job removing the stricken people. Therefore, as soon as Carry had given her address, the meeting was quickly ended.

The next day she tried to visit Mayor Harrison but was informed he was not in his office. Then, with newspaper reporters acting as tour guides, Carry visited a dozen downtown saloons, where she verbally attacked the bartenders and customers. The infamous hatchet was locked safely in her hotel room.

During the afternoon, an incident occurred that seems almost too coincidental and which hints of backstage maneuvering by a reporter seeking a good story. At 290 State Street, Carry entered a saloon belonging to John Juertick, which had "an extremely young man tending bar." She started to tell him that he was underage but stopped in midsentence and stared at him, amazed.

The young man grinned. "How are you, Grandma?"

The bartender was Riley White, the son of David's daughter Lola and Carry's grandson by marriage.

"Don't you remember me, Grandma?"

"Yes, I know you." Carry turned and slowly walked into the street. Riley ran after her. "We had a long talk and while he returned to his job, he promised to quit and take up temperance work," Carry told the reporters, tears streaking her cheeks.

The unexpected encounter with Riley had sapped Carry's famous energy and drive. Disheartened, she boarded a train for Topeka, where she still had to face trial. Arriving in that Kansas city on February 14, Carry wrote to Riley:

My Darling Riley:—I got here all right. O Chicago! Chicago! How fondly my heart turns to thee—the home of fond hearts that were so loving to me. . . . There is a better day for thee, Riley. Come to me as quickly as possible. I will be here until Tuesday morning at 11 o'clock when I go to Medicine Lodge. Your loving grandmother,

Carrie [sic] Nation

Riley White never went to Carry, nor did he quit his job and enlist in the temperance movement.

The strange misspelling of her own name at the end of that letter was a mistake that Carry would make often in her lifetime. She never offered a reason. Generally, the error occurred at highly emotional periods and may have had something to do with the fact that her father also occasionally lasped into the *-ie* spelling. At the time of Carry's birth, however, her name was written in the brass-clasped family Bible as *Carry*.

During Carry's absence the temper of Topeka had not cooled and, if anything, the city was approaching an eruption point. A Committee for Public Safety had been formed to warn jointists and to meet with government officials to be certain the state liquor law was enforced.

Upon her return, Carry set up an office and living quarters in a building she was later to buy and donate to the W.C.T.U. The furnishings were simple: a plain table, a dry-goods box for her personal items, and a few dishes and kitchen utensils. There was no carpet, no decorations, nothing to offset the monastic atmosphere of the small room.

"I used to delight in cut-glass, china, plush velvet and lace. Now I can say vanity of vanities, all is vanity."

From this office, Carry reentered the maelstrom by claiming the Committee of Public Safety was too passive and urging immediate attacks upon the shuttered joints and the warehouse where liquor and bar fixtures were stored. Her wishes were soon to become a reality.

February 17, 1901, was a day that Topekans would long remember. As early as six o'clock in the morning, pockets of antisaloonists formed at focal points in the city. One group contained male students from Washburn College who had constructed a three-hundred-pound battering ram from a peeled tree trunk. The weapon had oaken handholds spaced along its seven-foot length, and the tip was a poured-concrete head about the size of a barrel.

Before the police were able to clear the streets by nine o'clock that night, Carry had been arrested four times, two of those imprisonments ending when a black saloonist, Nick Chiles, put up bail for Carry.

"You're very kind to me," Carry said on the first occasion.

Chiles bowed and said he was pleased he could assist her.

"When I have time," she said, "I'll smash your joint, too."

One joint that was smashed that day was Edward Murphy's Unique Restaurant. Also thoroughly demolished were a livery stable containing liquor and bar apparatus and a cold-storage plant mistakenly believed to hold forbidden articles.

The following morning, Judge Z. T. Hazen remanded Carry to the county jail. Here, Carry was placed in a large room in the hospital ward, rather than in a cell.

She had a bed and two tables, and quickly arranged for a box to store her belongings. Actually the room was more pleasant than her own little office. During her stay, Carry transformed the cell room into a business office.

And business was booming. A telegram arrived offering her five hundred dollars a week to act in a temperance play. An even more generous proposition came from a circus owner, who suggested a high salary and her own private Pullman car if she would travel with the circus and deliver fifteen-minute speeches in the afternoons and evenings.

"Not yet, while I've still got some sense," she informed reporters. "I won't let myself be made a fool of even for a million dollars a minute."

Later Carry would reevaluate the stage as a suitable medium for her message, but now she decided to start her own temperance newsletter because "the Republican newspapers of Kansas, and other States were determined" to place her "in a false light before the people." She enlisted the help of her benefactor, Nick Chiles, who owned part interest in the printing firm that published the Kansas *Plaindealer*. David Nation came to Topeka to draw up the partnership papers.

The newspaper, which appeared on March 9, 1901, under the banner the *Smasher's Mail*, was basically a prohibition propaganda sheet, although Carry tried to maintain a balanced point of view. Each issue carried a dramatic editorial by Carry which, as the weeks went on, became vigorously outspoken. Also, under a section called "Hell Letters," later revised to "Letters from Hell," the newspaper printed opposing opinions.

For example, a man from San Luis Obispo, California, penned, "You have strength in your tongue and venom in your nails. I expect you'll be dead soon." And, in support of this fellow's expectation, a crank wrote: "To that Blockhead Carry Nation whose [sic] up in jail at Topeka: If you are so game, why don't you come to my saloon in Dallas you know better, ha, ha. I will break a Colt's .45 over your head and let my dogs gnash your skull bones."

Carry seemed impervious to these insults and threats, but she was becoming increasingly annoyed with Chiles, who kept toning down her editorials and a few of the more abusive letters. Unfortunately, when she checked the partnership papers drawn up by her husband, Carry found she had no legal rights to protect her writing. After three weeks, Carry claimed Chiles was "humiliating her" and broke off their business arrangement. Chiles later insisted he had backed out first, because he feared libel suits arising from Carry's vitriolic attacks on saloonists and politicians.

The *Smasher's Mail* was henceforth printed by the same company that published the *Kansas Farmer*. At first, Carry allowed David to edit the twice-weekly paper, but soon he was tampering with the contents even more than Nick Chiles had. Eventually, Carry would not allow David even to touch her correspondence, thus adding another item to David's own list of insults.

Meanwhile, as conducive as the jail's accommodations were for Carry's office work, she was extremely interested in accepting a speaking engagement in Peoria, Illinois. Mr. W. A. Brubaker, a prohibition lecturer, had promised her fifty dollars for her talk, and the Peoria *Journal* offered her an additional one hundred dollars if she would edit the newspaper the day she was in the city. What made this particular offer attractive was that Peoria was the world's largest manufacturing center of rye whiskey. Carry would, in effect, be bringing the battle to the enemy's citadel.

Unfortunately, Judge Hazen would not release Carry unless she posted bond, and to Carry such an action seemed equivalent to surrender. Finally, in a desperate attempt to be able to lecture in Peoria, Carry allowed several ministers to pay her bond "with the provision that on my return I be locked up again promptly and the bond withdrawn."

Her attack on the whiskey capital proved to be a disappointment. The speech went well, and a tour of the distilleries provided Carry with an opportunity to give reporters good copy, but her own copy for the Peoria *Journal* was ravaged.

Her editorial would have been an effective one because Carry was always talented with words, both in lectures and in print. "For instance," she originally wrote, "there is a sign, 'Old Crow Whiskey.' This is slandering the crow, for there is not a crow or vulture that will use a drop of this slop." And against the old Moore-family enemy, tobacco, she stated: "There are the 'Robert Burns' and 'Tom Moore' cigars. There was not a cigar in England when Burns or Tom Moore lived. . . . I never remember seeing the 'Grant Cigar,' by the way. His name is not used because he died with tobacco cancer."

Permitting her lecture manager, Brubaker, to take the finished copy to the newspaper, Carry eagerly awaited the publication of that day's edition. Upon reading the *Journal*, however, Carry discovered that Brubaker had altered her editorial drastically, even changing the meaning of most of her statements. Also, the newspaper bulged with ads for whiskey and tobacco.

118

Outraged, Carry released a statement that "this man Brubaker was posing as a prohibitionist, but he was as loyal to the cause as Judas was to Jesus." And with that remark, Carry headed back to Topeka and jail.

CHAPTER 12

Carry Nation's battle against alcohol had originated in a small Kansas town, but now her activities were national news. Her name flashed in headlines from Portland, Maine, to Portland, Oregon, and magazines such as *The Saturday Evening Post* printed illustrated articles about her exploits. Even children across the country were playing "saloon smashing." Boys would build saloon-forts and girls would attack the structures with stones and clubs.

Adults on both sides of the temperance question were becoming more militant, also. Mary Green of Boston pushed her way into a Cambridge Street bar, shouting, "I'm Carry Nation, and I'll leave no rumshop in this town," whereupon she picked up a free-lunch platter and threw it into the bartender's face. She then proceeded to "reduce the bar to molecules."

In New York City, Herman Procknow smashed the mirrors in Edward O'Brien's Third Avenue Bar, and a person claiming to be Carry Nation's brother kicked in the front-door panels of McMahon's Bar on East 138th Street.

Several women invaded a bar in Anderson, Indiana,

and one of the crusaders discovered her husband drinking in the establishment. She promptly whacked him with a board and dragged him home by his ear.

In Winfield, Kansas, antiprohibitionists invaded the United Brethren Church one night, smashing the stained-glass windows and the organ. An anonymous note was pinned to the cross. "We will show you how to treat the saloons, and will give you as good as you send. The next saloon in town wrecked means that some of you will be killed." The warning was not an empty one. Police arrested men sprinkling rat poison into the wells and cisterns of temperance leaders, and the homes of some antiliquor persons were set on fire.

And Carry Nation sat in a Topeka jail. Imprisonment was becoming a frustrating hindrance for Carry because she wanted to be out spreading the word and gathering new supporters. At last she allowed her brother, Campbell Moore of Kansas City, to put up the two-thousand-dollar bond for her release. She accompanied Campbell back to Kansas City for a brief rest, but soon resumed her mission at a frenetic pace.

First, she was invited to Leavenworth by members of the Old Soldier's Home, who claimed that every payday seventy half-barrels of beer were sold in the home. The rest home, however, was on federal property, and Carry was refused admittance.

From there she went to St. Louis, and was met at the Union Station by reporters, who led her to the corner of Sixteenth and Market Street, where Joseph Sauerburger's saloon now bore the name "The Carry Nation Bar."

"Take down that sign, my man, before I come back into this town," she ordered, "or I'll use a little hatchetation on you."

Her tour continued into Cincinnati and towns in

Kentucky, her home state. On April 2, she returned to St. Louis to deliver an hour-and-a-half-long speech and then set out for Sauerburger's bar. The sign was still in place. Pulling a hatchet from under her cape, Carry charged into the bar, but was met by Sauerburger, who waved a pistol at her. Carry was forced to leave the premises and leave the sign in place as well.

Next came a return to Kansas City and then to Wichita, where she was arrested on the old warrant from her January saloon smashing.

A few days later her brother, J. W. Moore, died in Louisburg, Kansas. Carry was released temporarily so she could attend his funeral. The death affected her deeply. Back in jail, she suffered spells of depression during which she could not eat and was able to sleep only a few hours each night. She prayed constantly, moving around in the small cell on her knees. At times she would deliver long, involved speeches to audiences only she saw.

David offered no help and was creating more aggravation by his statements to the press that he would never again live with his wife. Carry had forbidden him to have any association with her activities, although she was still paying his room and board.

Campbell Moore learned about his sister's deteriorating mental state and immediately posted bail so that she could visit his home for a period of recuperation. The rest was short because Carry had to return to Topeka District Court for her part in the February 17 riot.

Her friends were shocked when Carry entered a plea of insanity, though she probably had her reasons. The personal problems with David and the loss of her brother may have made further confinement seem intolerable. Also, as she later wrote a friend, jail was "becoming tiresome" and she was "spending about as much time in jail as out." Judge Hazen, however, told the jury to ignore the plea of insanity, and Carry was found guilty. She was released on bail until the sentencing.

Setting forth on a lecture circuit through the Middle West, Carry prospered as huge crowds gathered at each stop and she was able to do a thriving business in the sale of her tiny hatchets and the *Smasher's Mail.* On the Fourth of July, Carry appeared before an audience of eight-thousand people in Crawfordsville, Indiana. During her energetic speech, the platform collapsed, spilling Carry and the local dignitaries onto the ground. Carry sprained her ankle, but she wanted to continue her talk. The police, however, insisted that she receive medical attention.

Later that day she recruited about twenty boys and girls between ten and twelve years of age. Leading them down Crawfordsville's main street, she stopped before a saloon.

"Look, children, what is that place?"

"A hellhole," they replied.

"Anything else?"

"A murder shop."

"What do they sell?" Carry asked the youngsters.

"Hell-broth and devil-soup."

"What do they do?"

"They murder souls!"

"What must we do to such a place?"

The children chorused: "Smash it!"

Carry led the invasion as the youngsters shrieked with pleasure. The boys ran along the bar and sideboard, breaking glasses, bottles, and mirrors. The girls hacked away at the woodwork and the bar. The "hatchetation" lasted only minutes, but the devastation was thorough. Carry brought her troops into the street in search of another bar, but the children fled when the police arrived. The owner would not press charges, because Carry was the main attraction that day in Crawfordsville. His bar had acquired a degree of fame by being the only saloon in that small Indiana town to be wrecked by Carry Nation.

Like a Kansas tornado, Carry whirled from state to state, exciting the residents and, at times, leaving behind a trail of wreckage: St. Louis, Terre Haute, and Clarksburg, Ohio. While en route to Columbus, where she had still another lecture to deliver, Carry learned that David had filed for divorce on August 9. *The New York Times* quoted her reaction.

"I'm not much surprised. I've been looking for it. I married him twenty-five years ago in Holden, Missouri. My friends were opposed to it. All this time he has been an encumbrance upon me and I have no respect for him. Now that he is going his way, I'm rather glad of it. . . ."

In Columbus, Carry learned the charges that the seventy-three-year-old David was bringing against her: cruelty, desertion, subjecting him to humiliation, and stealing nine hundred dollars from his bank account. There was one last accusation, which was ridiculous. David claimed that Carry had stolen his feather bed.

"Lies!" snapped Carry when questioned by reporters. "He didn't have nine hundred dollars, and the feather bed was always mine. If it hadn't been for me, he would have had nothing."

And, with that response, the cyclone was spinning again, this time headed in an easterly direction for the first time in her campaign. A St. Lawrence River steamboat brought her to a Watertown, New York, meeting near the Canadian border. Then she traveled to Atlantic City, where she sold $2500 worth of her miniature hatchets and addressed an audience of five thousand people. From there, it was a short distance to New York City.

For her grand entrance into what she considered the wickedest city in the world, Carry wore a new alpaca dress and bonnet. A hatchet was strapped to her waist, and she lugged a shoulder bag filled with souvenir hatchets, campaign buttons, and issues of the *Smasher's Mail*. Welcomed at the train by numerous reporters and a large crowd, Carry was escorted to the Hotel Victoria on Fifth Avenue and Twenty-seventh Street. Her scrawling handwriting filled half the register page with "Carry Nation, Your Loving Home Defender." For her place of residence, she wrote simply, "Kansas."

The saloonkeepers of New York City had made their own preparations for Carry's onslaught. Most bars along Broadway and the Tenderloin (the midtown area) had hired extra guards. The Hoffman House Bar, which was only three blocks from Carry's hotel, had posted burly guards at every entrance. The owners feared that Carry might attempt to destroy the famous ten-thousand-dollar painting, "The Nymph and Satyrs," behind the bar. Other bartenders considered Carry's visit to their city as a cause for celebration. Several saloonkeepers invited Carry to their place of business, offering kegs and bottles for her to smash and promising to have reporters there so that her "hatchetation" would receive full coverage.

Late on the morning of her arrival, Carry stepped into an "open barouche drawn by a team of spirited black horses," and began a tour of the city. Acting Mayor Guggenheim claimed to be closeted with urgent city business, so Carry's first stop was to be the office of

Police Commissioner Michael C. Murphy. As the carriage took Carry down Fifth Avenue, cabs and hacks filled with reporters and the curious trailed after her. Each time the parade passed a saloon, Carry stood up and shouted, "Rummies! Murderers! Hellholes!"

The New York City Police Department was already under heavy public criticism for corruption, so the arrival of Carry Nation at the Mulberry Street headquarters was not appreciated.

At one point, Commissioner Murphy told Carry, "You ought to go back to Kansas and stay there."

"Are you angry with me, my dear father, because I want all these rum-holes closed?"

"What the devil do you mean, madam? I am not your father."

"I know it," Carry said softly. "But you look it. You're old enough to be my father. I'm fifty-five, and you're eighty-five if you're a day."

Leaving the police commissioner livid, Carry sauntered along Bleecker Street as several hundred people followed her. A reporter informed her that the ex-prize-fight champion, John L. Sullivan, who now operated his own bar, had told people, "If that old woman ever comes around my place, I'll throw her down the sewer."

"Take me to his saloon," ordered Carry.

Sullivan was relaxing in front of his Forty-second Street establishment when Carry's barouche rounded the corner from Broadway. Taking one look at Carry, hatchet in hand, Sullivan quickly vanished inside the building. Alighting from the carriage, Carry sent her card in to Sullivan. The reply was that Mr. Sullivan was asleep in his upstairs quarters and could not be disturbed.

"Well, just tell him I'll be back, and then we'll see if he'll stick me in a sewer hole."

CARRY NATION

As the barouche clattered away, Sullivan was seen peeking from an upstairs window. Ironically, years later he would be converted to Carry's cause and become an active temperance crusader himself.

Carry left the city for a speaking engagement in College Corner, Ohio, but before the saloonkeepers of New York City could sigh with relief, she was on her way back.

The morning after her second arrival, *The New York Times* summed up Carry's return: "Mrs. Carrie [sic] Nation arrived in New York yesterday morning. Before the day was over she had attended St. Patrick's Cathedral, made an effort to penetrate the interior of the Democratic Club, toured the Tenderloin, been arrested on Eighth Avenue, and delivered a lecture at Carnegie Hall on the subject, 'The Lord's Saloon.'"

Carry had a contract to appear at the Steeplechase Park in Coney Island. Beginning September 3, Carry was to speak twice daily for ten days. Though lecturing at the honky-tonk stretch in Brooklyn was criticized by many temperance leaders, Carry figured people who would not ordinarily have heard her might be attracted by sheer curiosity. In this way she might gather a few unexpected disciples. On Labor Day—in the midst of belly dancers, dizzying amusement-park rides, and beer gardens—Carry mounted a platform.

"Coney Island would not be what it is were it not for the government of New York," she told the audience. "What can you expect of a government run by a lot of beer-smeared, nicotine-faced, beak-nosed devils?"

Everyone applauded. On this particular occasion she had completely won over the listeners. That would not be the case a few days later.

From the very beginning of her saloon smashing, one of the politicians she had singled out most for criti-

127

cism was President William McKinley. Frequently in lectures and in her editorials for the *Smasher's Mail* she had labeled McKinley as "the Brewers' President."

While attending the Pan-American Exposition in Buffalo on September 6, President McKinley was shot in the abdomen by an anarchist, Leon Czolgosz. With the bullet still inside his body, McKinley lingered in critical condition for days. Republicans and Democrats alike were horrified by the deed, and public sentiment on the President's behalf was strong. In Casper, Wyoming, Hans Wagner, the baseball player known as the Flying Dutchman, spoke in defense of Czolgosz, with the result that Wagner was tarred and feathered and run out of town on a rail. There was much talk that if the President should die, Lake Superior, Pike's Peak, and even Washington, D.C., should be renamed in his honor.

On September 8, while McKinley lay dying, someone asked Carry during one of her Coney Island talks, "How about the President now?"

"I shed no tears for this McKinley," Carry answered. "I had no sympathy for this friend of the brewers, neither have I any sympathy for this assassin—"

The audience roared its disapproval, and when Carry tried to speak, hisses and catcalls drowned out her words.

"Shut up, you sots," Carry cried. "My loyalty to the homes of America demands that I denounce such a President and his crowd."

Bags of peanuts and popcorn and wads of newspaper were hurled at her. The crowd began to chant, "Lynch her, lynch her," but then the people rushed from the meeting, cheering for President McKinley.

CARRY NATION

The New York Times of September 9, 1901, badly misquoted Carry. According to the newspaper, Carry had said she was "glad President McKinley had been murderously assaulted and hoped he would die." Also, that "a friend of rum-sellers and brewers does not deserve to live."

The garbled account was reprinted by other newspapers, and the next day a wave of resentment against Carry began building up at a frightening rate. The owner of Steeplechase Park canceled her contract, and Carry's manager rushed her off on a tour of upper New York State.

But word had already reached the hinterlands. A lecture in Albany, New York, ended abruptly when the audience stormed the stage, driving Carry into an alley, where she was stoned. The next week she spoke in Elmira, New York, and had to climb into a farmer's wagon because an angry mob was bearing down on her. The series of talks was hastily concluded in Rochester a few weeks later, and Carry returned to Medicine Lodge.

More trouble awaited her in Kansas. On November 27, 1901, Judge Gilette, considering David's divorce suit, found Carry guilty of "gross neglect of duty and desertions," but not of "cruelty." Carry would receive no alimony, and the property was divided equally, with Carry being given the house in which she first realized her life's mission.

And then came another court appearance in Topeka, for which she was fined one hundred dollars and sentenced to thirty days for wrecking the livery stable on February 17. After two weeks, however, the governor pardoned her.

But the zest was gone. After a meteoric rise, her

success appeared to have peaked, and her activities seemed repetitious, like echoes of past glories. Thus, at the age of fifty-six, divorced but world-famous, Carry Nation cast about for a way to bring the magic back into her crusade.

CHAPTER 13

One avenue seemed to offer exciting possibilities, and that was the college circuit. Remembering the Washburn students who had constructed the battering ram for the Topeka raid, Carry decided to accept more invitations from colleges across the United States. Perhaps by doing so, she would find an untapped supply of new converts. She had already appeared at several Midwestern colleges and had been pleased with the spontaneous cheers her speeches had elicited whenever she denounced tobacco and alcohol. What Carry may not have considered was that a majority of these schools had been nonsecular institutions whose students already had a predilection for antivice campaigns.

An invitation had come from Mr. W. B. Burris, who claimed his student group at the University of Missouri wished to raise money for the W.C.T.U. With hopes soaring, Carry set off for Columbia, Missouri. She was in fine form and delivered one of her most forceful assaults against liquor. The people who attended her talk were avowed prohibitionists; the people who had organized the meeting were confirmed drinkers. Mr. Burris, known as "Bottle Bill" to friends and fellow students, used the large profits from Carry's appearance to buy champagne.

Undaunted by the deceit, Carry next visited the Woolley Club on the University of Michigan campus in Ann Arbor. Here she was given a banquet and a "heartfelt" reception. "It gave me a new life to look at such men of intellectual and moral force. . . . These are the hatchets that will smash up evil and build up good. . . . God will bless the Woolley Club of Ann Arbor and their kind."

The Carry Nation college addresses received wide newspaper exposure which, in turn, brought in even more invitations. A flurry of letters from Yale caught Carry's interest. One boy wrote that there was so much brandy in his food at the Yale mess hall that the meals made him dizzy and this had a negative effect on his marks. Another student enclosed sample menus, which listed dishes such as Roast Ham and Champagne Sauce, Apple Dumpling with Brandy Sauce and, as a beverage, Claret Wine Punch. Immediately, Carry canceled a scheduled lecture and headed east.

Carry arrived in New Haven on September 29, 1902, and went straight to the mayor's office, where a secretary informed her that Mayor Studly had no jurisdiction over the policies of Yale University. Leaving the building, Carry encountered the Yale Jolly Eight Club, the membership of which contained some of Yale's heaviest drinkers. Leading her across the Green to the nearby university, the Jolly Eights brought her to a spot where a mob of cheering students waited to greet her. A well-rehearsed glee club sang, "Good morning, Carry. . . . Been a-dreaming about you, my pretty maid." This was the first hint of what sort of day Carry had before her.

CARRY NATION

Carry mounted the steps of Osborn Hall, but whenever she tried to speak, the students drowned her out with cheers or lusty versions of drinking songs and temperance melodies such as "Down With King Alcohol" and "Good-Bye Booze." She stood there forty-five minutes unable to penetrate the din with a single word.

Finally, she turned angrily to a nearby student. "What's the matter with these rummies? Don't they want to hear me?"

"They're drunk," the boy replied. "They had ham with rum champagne sauce for lunch and haven't gotten over it yet."

Dismayed by this seemingly undeniable evidence of university-induced drunkenness, Carry hurried to see President Dr. Arthur T. Hadly. After listening to her complaints of college food doused with alcohol, Dr. Hadley calmly explained that the boys were fooling her. The cooking additives were merely fruit juices with fancy names or "bad vinegar."

Later that day while Carry was at Mory's Restaurant, a famous undergraduate hangout, several members of the Jolly Eight asked her to pose for a photograph. Surrounded by students, she stretched out one arm and held a glass of water in the other. As the photographer was about to click the shutter, the boys pulled out beer mugs and bottles. And when the print was developed, Carry's water glass had turned into a goblet of foaming beer and her uplifted hand held a cigarette.

That night when reporters questioned Carry in New York City, she publicly stated that the Yale boys were "the toughest proposition I have ever met." Yale, she said, was "a school of vice to a great extent."

Privately, she told friends that she thought the doctored photograph, which now graces the bar of the New York City Yale Club, was a good joke even if it was at her expense. This ability to laugh at herself was one of the characteristics that made Carry Nation stand above the hundreds of other self-righteous temperance crusaders of those years. Her sense of humor enabled her to talk with people of all levels in a relaxed, friendly way. Her quickness with words usually defeated balky public officials or saloonists and, at the same time, made good newspaper copy.

Her next appearance at an institution of higher learning was at the University of Texas at Austin. On October 16, 1902, Carry was greeted at the train by "Uncle Tom" Murrah, a "fine type of old-fashioned gentleman." Before going to the university, Carry and Murrah visited Bill Davis's saloon at Congress Avenue and Fifth Street.

As soon as Davis spotted Carry and Murrah entering the bar, he ordered both of them to get out.

"Do you know who you're talking to? I'm Carry Nation, and I was never known to leave a saloon until I got good and ready."

Carry pulled out her hatchet, but Davis got a grip on her neck and arm and pushed her into the street. Carry then began making a speech at the front entrance of the saloon, but Davis placed the large horn of a phonograph in an opened window. The blaring music defeated Carry's vocal efforts, but she wouldn't give up. The police finally intervened in the noise contest, but "Uncle Tom" Murrah persuaded them not to place Carry under arrest.

At the campus, a hundred cheering students met Carry and escorted her to the main building, but nervous school officials would not let her enter. Therefore, Carry simply turned around and began speaking from the steps.

"I heard a voice by my side . . . there stood Principal Presley Prather. He was white with excitement. . . . 'Madam, we do not allow such!' "

Carry told him, "I am speaking for the good of these boys."

"We do not allow speaking on the campus."

"I have spoken to the students at Ann Arbor and Yale, and I will speak to the boys of Texas!"

The jubilant students shouted their encouragement. The uproar frightened a passing mailman's horse, causing the postal vehicle to veer and smash into a tree. Letters and papers and postcards flew in all directions. Although Carry offered to pay the damages, the mailman refused, claiming the harm done to his wagon was minor. Everybody laughed except the college president. The mail service had been only temporarily interrupted, but unfortunately, Carry's Austin lecture was ended.

Her final college speech was supposed to take place at Harvard, and her treatment on the Cambridge campus was similar to her reception at Yale, so she was unable even to begin the talk. She left Boston for Springfield, Massachusetts, determined to abandon the college scene, because she already had a new field of endeavor. First, however, she took a parting swipe at the Ivy League schools.

"The great controversy between Yale and Harvard now is which shall excel in brute force, and football seems to be the test. Colleges were founded for the purpose of educating the young, on moral, intellectual, and spiritual lines. . . . It used to be conceded that the mind made the man. Now the forces of the mule and ox are preferred."

On November 17, 1902, Carry entered an arena that years before she had insisted "a million dollars a minute" would not be sufficient enticement. The theater. And, to the disgust of many of her associates, Carry did not choose the legitimate theater of drama for her debut but rather the world of burlesque. Her opening night came in Springfield midway through the final act of a burlesque show. There were hecklers that night, and during most of her shows on the circuit, but these men forgot that they were dealing with the woman who had sent John L. Sullivan scurrying for safety.

Carry used three methods of silencing the drunks and the show-offs in the audience. First, she would continue speaking, simply increasing her volume. If this technique didn't work, she would lower her voice to a whisper, so only the front row could hear her. Generally, everyone quickly quieted down. A few people enjoyed baiting Carry, but in truth, all of them wanted to hear what she would say next. For the very obstreperous members out front, she would hurl back insults and threats in such colorful language that the hecklers would stop, shocked that a woman knew and used such words.

Carry justified her theatrical appearances by claiming to be the sole temperance crusader who would be accepted by burlesque audiences. "I got hundreds of calls to go on the stage before I did. Gradually, I saw the light. This was the largest missionary field in the world. No one ever got a call or was allowed to go there except Carry Nation. The door was never opened to anyone but me. The hatchet opened it."

At about this time, a new game was becoming popular throughout the country. The guessing contests took place in homes, bars, and railroad coaches. To win, a person had to anticipate where Carry Nation would turn up next because, aside from her scheduled performances, no one ever knew where she would appear. Certainly, the socialites attending the Madison Square

Garden horse show on November 20, 1902, did not expect to see Carry sitting in the gallery. Nor did they anticipate her moving down to the Vanderbilt box, where she instructed Mrs. Alfred Gwynne Vanderbilt and her woman friends on the appropriateness of their evening gowns.

"You think you're well dressed," Carry shouted at the ladies. "But you ought to be ashamed of yourself for wearing such disgraceful clothes. Take them off at once and dress yourself more modestly."

Alfred Gwynne Vanderbilt returned to the box during Carry's harangue and ordered the attendants to remove her. Unwisely, they brought Carry to the Garden Café at the corner of Madison Avenue and Twenty-seventh Street, and she caused another scene there. Now the police had to be summoned to remove Carry.

Early in December, 1902, Carry returned to Topeka, where she took "elocution" and acting lessons while working on a play, *War on Drink,* in which she planned to perform the leading role. Taking the play manuscript and the first pages of her autobiography, *The Use and Need of the Life of Carry Nation,* Carry journeyed to Los Angeles to appear at an amusement park called The Chutes. While there she made a side trip that must have outwitted those trying to determine where she would next make a disturbance: Carry invaded the California legislature. Then, on the way back to Kansas, she stopped briefly in Salt Lake City, Utah, and asked a leader of the Mormon Church to allow her to speak in the Tabernacle.

"Do you wish to become a Mormon, madam?" the man asked.

"No, I want to see a polygamist. Show me one, and I'll brand him with my hatchet."

When the plans to produce her own play collapsed,

Carry accepted a contract to play the stricken mother of a drunken son in *Ten Nights in a Bar Room*. At her suggestion, the title was changed to *Hatchetation*, the name of another of her unsuccessful plays, and the last act was rewritten to include a saloon-smashing scene. Like all talented actresses, Carry began to live the part. The reviews the next day noted that she destroyed twenty-nine liquor bottles and forty-four glasses, and overturned four chairs. In truth, she became so involved that she nearly demolished all the scenery as well as the backstage area of the Elizabeth, New Jersey, theater.

On December 14, 1903, the play moved to the Third Avenue Theater in New York City, so that Carry was thereby competing with well-known performers such as Ethel Barrymore acting in *Cousin Kate* at the Harlem Opera House and Frank O'Connor onstage at the Princess Theater. In the eyes of the newspaper reviewers, however, Carry lost the competition.

The early-morning edition of the New York *Tribune* reported that Carry was not to be taken seriously as an actress. "There is no reason why Mrs. Nation's advent on the stage should cause Sarah Bernhardt to shake in her boots or Mrs. Fiske to tremble."

Though the drama critics were cool to her theatrical efforts, Carry was most enthusiastic and less than a month later she was appearing at a Philadelphia theater, where she lectured between the acts of the play, *The Heart of a Hero*.

The following May Carry made a brief visit to Canada, where she delivered three speeches and sold all her miniature hatchets. She would have preferred touring more provinces, but she had a contract to appear in a Chicago theater. Reluctantly, she prepared to return to the United States though she promised her Canadian fans that she would soon return. While appearing in the Chicago variety theater, which had a connecting museum, Carry was angered to learn that many American newspapers were erroneously reporting that she was earning three hundred dollars a week to pose in a museum and be gawked at by paying customers.

In June, she reentered Canada and visited the Maritime Provinces, where she was well received. She labeled the residents of Prince Edward Island as "the most intelligent and moral people, as a body, I have ever met." The picturesque fields, the quaint, shingled houses, and the small, plump horses all appealed to her. Also, figuring prominently in Carry's positive reaction was the fact that Prince Edward Island had recently legalized prohibition. The only legal drinking establishment in the whole province was The Club in Charlottetown, the capital. The reason for this solitary exception was that the Premier had insisted that The Club remain open, or he would veto the law or else enforce it feebly if at all.

As Carry traveled on through Canada, her lectures were poorly attended because many Canadians had believed the accounts that claimed Carry had allowed herself to become a museum piece in Chicago. The Canadian press printed her offer to pay a reward of fifty dollars to any individual who had ever seen her in a museum. This assuaged the dismayed people, and her tour became increasingly popular.

Then came more speeches in the United States: Elizabethtown, Kentucky, and Medicine Lodge. When the invitation came from the town where Carry's mission had started, her spiritual home, she eagerly accepted. Frankly, she was tired and needed to replenish her physical and spiritual energy.

CARRY NATION

On February 15, 1905, five years from the day she had planned the attack on O. L. Day's drugstore, Carry stepped off the train in Medicine Lodge and gazed around expectantly for her friends and comrades. But no one was there. As the train chugged away, Carry picked up her suitcases and trudged toward the station bus.

CHAPTER 14

F amily problems were once again to drain a portion of Carry's energy when, in the fall of 1905, she received a letter from Charlien's husband saying his wife had been judged insane and the only recourse he had was to place Charlien in an asylum. Carry was in the East at the time, involved in still another lecture tour. When she received Alexander McNab's letter, her old fear of hospitals and mental institutions was revived. She wrote Alexander at once, begging him not to commit Charlien until her current series of public appearances was completed and she could come to Texas. McNab did not wait, however, and had Charlien institutionalized in a private hospital. He had all the bills forwarded to Carry.

Finally, Carry's last contracted speaking date was fulfilled and she hurried to San Antonio. "When I went there I saw she [Charlien] was not a subject for the insane asylum. I telephoned her husband at Richmond and said to him, 'I want my child, let me take her, I will be responsible.' He refused . . . and I was powerless to take her away. I called him again and said 'I will not pay her expenses here any longer.' "

141

McNab at once notified the head of the San Antonio sanatorium to transfer Charlien to the state asylum. Carry went to Austin, but the superintendent of the state hospital informed her that although the hospital was not a fitting place for Charlien, Alexander McNab had forbidden him to allow Charlien to leave with Carry. "He advised me to let her stay there a month, then I could [legally] come and take my child away. I did this and got my child in my own possession."

Charlien traveled by herself to Oklahoma, where Carry met her, and they both continued on to Hot Springs, Arkansas. Charlien needed constant attention due to her uncontrollable desire for alcohol. Carry had to watch her every minute of the day, and at night she dared not sleep for fear Charlien would try to sneak off to obtain liquor. Carry could not spend all her time supervising Charlien, however, for the numerous court fines and travel expenses had practically depleted her financial resources. When a contract to tour Texas was offered to her, Carry accepted the deal without hesitation even though she was fifty-nine years old and needed rest herself. But off she went. Meanwhile, she paid a qualified person to watch Charlien and tried to sell as many miniature hatchets as possible, as well as copies of a new temperance magazine she had recently started, the *Hatchet*.

The *Hatchet* was to involve Carry in a federal suit for "dispatching obscene material through the U.S. Mails." In 1906, a law labeled obscene and unmailable any written material that mentioned sex, venereal disease, or masturbation. In the July 1906 issue of the *Hatchet*, Carry had penned an editorial in the form of a letter "to little boys in which I warned them against the vice of self-abuse, telling them the consequences of such a dangerous practice."

A segment of Carry's supporters was incensed by the article. One man wrote, "I have always been one of your admirers, helping you all I can, but I cannot endorse your letter to 'the boys.' . . . It was unfit for even for me to read and is a hindrance to the good cause for which you stand." Another person claimed the editorial was a "blueprint for masturbation."

Receiving numerous complaints, the postal authorities investigated the magazine and declared the issue to contain obscene material. At the time, Carry was lecturing in Texas, so when the federal summons was delivered stating she was subject to criminal prosecution and must return to Guthrie, Oklahoma, for trial, she ignored the paper. The government dispatched a United States marshal to arrest Carry.

"I was in the depot at Celburne, Texas, when a very nice old gentleman whispered to me, 'I want to speak to you. I am a United States Marshal.' "

"I understand and I am ready to go with you," Carry told him.

Marshal R. M. Walden gave Carry the option of having her trial in Guthrie or Dallas. Hoping it would intrude less upon her speaking engagements, Carry chose Dallas. Walden and Carry boarded a train for that city.

During the ride, Carry befriended two Dallas men, who became upset when they learned that she was under arrest. They vowed that they would post bond for her as soon as they arrived in Dallas. The promise was valid. The train arrived in Dallas at nine o'clock that night, and the two men immediately went to the home of the United States Commissioner to arrange for Carry's release. The bond was paid, and Carry was allowed to leave Dallas the next morning to conclude the lecture tour. The only provision was that she must return in

September for the trial. Carry agreed to the stipulation because she badly needed the income from the speaking engagements.

However, Carry almost did not attend the federal trial because while she was in Denver, she was arrested for creating a disturbance. Fortunately for Carry, the mayor intervened and she was released.

The government had transported their witnesses from Guthrie, but Carry had to pay the expenses of her one character witness, the Reverend Charles Mitchell. When the court convened, the federal attorney read the charges and then carefully studied Carry's editorial. At length, he dismissed the charges, claiming the article was no more offensive than many passages of the Holy Writ. In fact, he seemed angered by the silliness of the case.

Though the charges had been ridiculous, the financial losses were serious. The legal expenses, Carry's own hotel and train bills, plus the bad publicity, which had caused several cancellations of lecture dates, all cut into her funds at a time when she was struggling to support herself and her alcoholic daughter.

She quickly accepted an offer to speak in Trinidad, Colorado, because the invitation was an opportunity to replenish some of the lost money. While in Trinidad, Carry spied a saloon that was doing a prosperous business. When she invaded the premises, however, the burly bartender threw her out with such force that Carry sprawled into the gutter. The jolt caused her to swallow her false teeth. She coughed them up again, but the teeth fell onto the pavement and broke. For the next several weeks she could swallow only liquids.

Weakened physically by the lack of solid food and drained emotionally by her tribulations, Carry thrashed about for a solution. Again, she entered a long period of prayer, fervently seeking heavenly guidance. One night, when Charlien was exhibiting improved self-control, Carry managed to obtain a few hours of badly needed sleep. In the darkness of her bedroom, the same voice that had instructed her to go to Kiowa spoke once more. "Go to Washington. On to Washington," the gentle voice bade her.

Carry had entertained thoughts about moving her center of operations to the nation's capital ever since her difficulty with the postal authorities. Now the old idea gained new urgency. In Washington, she could bring pressure upon the country's government, which possessed the power to enact legislation concerning the national temperance question. She decided, "We have been cutting off the tail of the serpent long enough. We must smash the viper on its head. It is in Washington. There is where the mischief began, there is where the mischief continues, there is where the mischief must be stopped."

Carry arrived in Washington early in 1907 and placed Charlien in Dr. Richard Gundy's private sanatorium. She had chosen the hospital on the basis of its excellent reputation, although she was still uncertain how she would be able to afford the medical bills. Obviously, the answer lay in her crusade: hatchet sales, subscriptions to the *Hatchet* and, most important, personal appearances.

When temperance and religious workers visited Carry and asked what they might do to help the cause, she said, "Get me a place to speak."

The request was not a simple one. Carry had already tried several mission houses, but they were either too small or would not let her appear in their halls. Next, she attempted to obtain an auditorium, but when the managers discovered Carry Nation would be the speaker, they rejected the rental fee. Her friends suggested Convention Hall, which seated seven thousand people and could be hired for $150 a day.

"That's out of the question," Carry told them. "All I've got is a hundred and seventy-five dollars in cash."

Weighing the matter further, Carry decided to risk everything on the drawing power of her name. The co-workers hired Convention Hall but, at Carry's request, did not tell the officials the name of the lecturer. Using what little money she had left, Carry ordered small cards printed as advertisements:

I speak at Convention Hall next Sunday at 3:30 to men only; also at night at 7:30 to everybody.

You are cordially invited.

Your loving "Home Defender,"
CARRY A. NATION

The legion of her friends and co-workers scattered the cards in hotels, stores, and saloons throughout the Washington, D.C., area. Carry came to Convention Hall that day knowing she had mere pennies to her name. The afternoon audience contained eight hundred men, which was encouraging, but the evening crowd, which almost filled the immense hall, was an answer to her prayers.

There was also an unexpected bonus. After her talk, a man about sixty years old who had "a good kind face" approached her. He said, "Had I known where you were when they first put you in jail, I would have sent you fifty dollars, for the smashing in Kansas was the greatest move ever made against the liquor traffic."

Though she had received many compliments over the years, this one, following an evening that had seen her financial salvation, was especially welcome.

"It's still not too late to help me," she informed him.

The gentleman offered her an apartment free of rent for five years. The residence would be a refuge for Carry often and had perfect facilities for her headquarters. Not only did she now have an ample office, but the apartment contained two bedrooms, a dining room, and a kitchen.

During the summer of 1906, Carry went about starting her campaign in this new setting. The *Hatchet* appeared regularly now, and the subscription lists grew daily. Though she refrained from any saloon smashing, Carry did hold prayer meetings and often verbally threatened Washington bartenders.

Then, at the end of July, sixty-year-old Carry began a new rash of lectures with the energy characteristic of her initial public appearances. Traveling through North Carolina, she spoke in eight cities, concluding the tour in Durham. The personal appearances brought in funds that were vitally needed, because Charlien's hospital bills were high. In addition, Carry continued to donate to organizations such as the W.C.T.U. and the Salvation Army.

When Carry returned to Washington, she was arrested in the post office for "drawing a crowd." The judge ordered her to pay a fine or face imprisonment in the women's workhouse.

Pausing only a moment, Carry said resolutely, "I have paid my last fine."

Sentenced to the workhouse, Carry entered the life almost agreeably. "When the day came to do my scrubbing, I got my bucket, scrubbing brush, soap and cloth and got down on my knees like the rest and did my scrubbing. . . . I never allowed myself to murmur and complain at anything . . . for my fellow prisoners were in a worse position than I."

Five days later The Holiness Association of Evansville, Indiana, wired enough money to pay her fine, and Carry was freed. But release did not mean rest. At once, she embarked on a new lecture tour, stopping in Evansville to thank her friends for the fine money. From there she went on to Muskogee, which was then in Indian territory. More cities waited to hear Carry Nation, more arduous train trips, and still more bills. The tour was a long and exhausting experience, but upon her arrival back in Washington, Carry learned she would have to be on the move once more.

The State Department notified her that a cousin, the son of her Aunt Hope, had been declared insane in Mexico. No one else in the family would have anything to do with the young man, so Carry traveled to Guadalajara, Mexico. The man was penniless when Carry found him, but he was not violent, so she persuaded him to accompany her back to Missouri, where she entered him in the state institution.

Now Carry had to attend to her own affairs. She went to the national Prohibition Party Convention in Columbus, Ohio, as the delegate from Washington, D.C. While there she met the organizing secretary of the Prohibition party of Dundee, Scotland, who suggested she ought to visit the British Isles. The prospect of speaking to an international audience appealed to Carry, so she set about lining up speaking engagements under the auspices of Scottish and English temperance societies. The arrangement provided that Carry would pay her own expenses in return for two thirds of the ticket sales. At least she hoped to recoup her expense money.

CARRY NATION

On November 28, 1908, Carry sailed on the *Columbia*, which was bound for Glasgow. Her traveling companion was Miss Callie Moore, a niece from Kansas City, who told reporters that "as soon as I get a little more courage I hope to smash something in a saloon."

Callie Moore never destroyed even one glass, but Carry had a hectic three months, and at the end of the tour had barely enough money to pay for her return ticket. As she disembarked in New York, reporters asked her opinion of Great Britain. Her only positive remark about England was that "the people do not chew gum. In that America could well imitate them."

While Carry was away the value of some property she owned in Oklahoma had increased tremendously after that territory became a state. Carry sold the land and invested the money "in a tract of land in the Ozark Mountains about thirty-five miles from Eureka Springs [Arkansas]." A small cottage was built on the property, which she called "Highland Farm Home" in honor of her Highland Scots ancestry. The cottage was to be her haven, the final hidden ledge where she could gaze out over the world and put her thoughts in order.

The date for this peaceful retirement, however, was a nebulous one, for Carry, who was already exhausted from the extensive speaking tour in Great Britain, was booked for thirty lectures during the summer of 1909.

CHAPTER 15

For the next year, Carry continued to lecture, and she even engaged in a few sessions of "hatchetation," as if she didn't want to get out of practice. In November 1909, she was arrested for invading the Knickerbocker Hotel bar in New York City. As always when Carry was around, a crowd collected and tied up traffic for half an hour. Her fine was only ten dollars.

Suddenly, she reappeared in Washington, D.C., and smashed the bar in the Union Station. This time the penalty was a bit more stiff: one hundred dollars.

The residents of Butte, Montana, listened to a Carry Nation lecture and then saw a Carry Nation performance when Carry became involved in a fight with Mrs. May Maloy, who ran a local dance hall and café. Carry had attempted to destroy a nude picture, which hung in the café.

But Carry was now sixty-three years old. For ten years she had suffered beatings by saloonists, repeated imprisonments in barely livable jails, and perpetual enervating platform appearances. No matter how strong an individual is, time and conditions wear down the human body. And so it was with Carry Nation. Returning to the small cottage in Arkansas that spring, she rested up for still another lengthy summer lecture tour. But the talks that summer lacked her usual fire and brimstone, and seemed mere imitations of her former speeches. Worse, she constantly paused, as she had difficulty finding the right word or constructing coherent sentences. In the midst of the tour, Carry became too exhausted to continue and had to abandon the schedule and return to Arkansas.

Carry spent the fall of 1910 in Arkansas and celebrated her sixty-fourth birthday there with a few friends. To outsiders, Carry appeared to be robust, but she was concerned about her health. Her eyes were troubling her and she could no longer read her Bible. At other times she experienced frightening lapses of memory, when she forgot people she knew well or was not able to remember what she had done the previous hour.

Carry, however, was not ready to give up. That winter she accepted a few speaking engagements in northern Arkansas, as if determined to prove that her physical infirmities could be overcome in the same manner she had put the jointists on the run.

On January 13, 1911, she spoke to an audience in Eureka Springs, Arkansas. At first the words flowed smoothly, and her talk had steely glints of the old Carry Nation. Members of the audience later remarked that she had seemed encouraged, pleased that she was winning this battle against time.

But soon the words came haltingly. Then she stopped, a confused expression on her face. She lifted a hand to her cheek, and people moved forward to help her to a seat. Refusing their assistance, she stood a few moments, gazing out over the audience.

Then, slowly, in a barely audible voice, she said, "I have done what I could."

Staggering a few steps, Carry collapsed into the arms of a friend.

The next morning, Carry was helped aboard a train and brought to the Evergreen Hospital in Leavenworth, Kansas. For five months, her weakened body clung to life even though the stroke she had suffered had left Carry listless and inert.

On June 2, 1911, a doctor and nurse stood near her bed. Softly, the doctor told Carry that her time was near. Carry smiled gently and then closed her eyes forever.

When Carry Nation was buried beside her mother in Belton, Missouri, only a few close friends were there to mourn. For years her grave remained unmarked. Then in 1924, friends collected money for a small granite shaft. At first, they had trouble locating the grave in the weeds and underbrush of the cemetery. The marker, which was erected on May 30, 1924, bears the words:

CARRY A. NATION
Faithful to the Cause of Prohibition
"She Hath Done What She Could"

There are few physical reminders of Carry Nation left today. The Dix River plantation is now nothing more than a few crumbling rock foundations in an overgrown field, which neighbors think may or may not have been the George Moore property. The Belton, Missouri, farm received some publicity during Prohibition, when federal agents discovered the new owners operating one of the largest stills ever found in that part of Missouri. The stream that flowed through the cool underground grotto where Carry had spent so many lonely hours was used to feed the still.

The yellow brick house in Medicine Lodge where Carry first received the message to sally forth against apparently unbeatable odds is now a museum maintained by the W.C.T.U.. A few mementos of Carry Nation are on display: several gold hatpins, a cracked brown leather valise, and a hatchet, now wired together lest it fall apart from age.

In Wichita, the Hotel Carey is long gone, as is a monument erected on the spot where Carry Nation was first arrested. This memorial, a handsomely inscribed fountain, was smashed by a runaway beer truck.

Even worse has been the damage done to Carry Nation's image over the years. Today, in the entertainment media and even in literature, she is presented as a campy, comic character, a crank with a penchant for vandalism. Carry Nation did have her flaws. Certainly, she never understood alcoholism in its true biological and psychological aspects, as people are beginning to view the problem today. Perhaps, in her forthright approach, however, she did manage to get to the heart of the situation. After all, the only way a person can stop being an alcoholic is to stop drinking alcohol.

Whether or not we agree with Carry Nation's goals and methods, there is no denying that she must rank as one of the important makers of our nation. Though the Anti-Saloon League was to take the credit for bringing about Prohibition in the United States, in truth, they only built upon the strong public awareness that Carry Nation had dramatically created. Today Kansas is still a dry state, and that is a direct result of Carry Nation's mission.

For all her weaknesses, Carry Nation must be admired for the inner courage with which she faced an often tragic life, for her compassion for those in need of help, and for her undeniable spiritual integrity.

As she lay near death, Carry confided to a friend: "I have made many grievous mistakes. They were of the head, not of the heart."

SELECTED BIBLIOGRAPHY

Asbury, Herbert, *Carry Nation*. New York, Alfred Knopf, 1929.

Beals, Carleton, *Cyclone Carry*. Philadelphia, Chilton Company, 1962.

Lee, Henry, *How Dry We Were*—Prohibition Revisited. Englewood Cliffs, New Jersey, Prentice-Hall, Inc., 1963.

Nation, Carry A., *The Use and Need of the Life of Carry A. Nation*. Topeka, Kansas, F. M. Steves & Sons, 1904.

Taylor, Robert Lewis, *Vessel of Wrath*, New York, The New American Library, Inc., 1966.

INDEX

157

160

161

162